"A gentle, thorough, easy-to-read guide for all of us who want to enter the ministry of Jesus setting the prisoners free. I enthusiastically recommend this book."

Carol Wimber, Vineyard Christian Fellowship

"A valuable tool for Christian ministry and a hands-on resource for anyone interested in this important subject or who has experienced the destruction connected with satanic manifestations. Its ideas and methods for handling this plaguing reality are biblical, practical and easy to follow. It is highly readable and conceptually clear. You will return to its insights over and over."

Bishop C. Milton Grannum, Ed.D., Ph.D., pastor, New Covenant Church of Philadelphia

"A thought-provoking book that deserves our attention and our meditation. Neal Lozano is not naïve; he knows the awful reality of human mental illness. But he is also attempting to give this spiritual battle the attention it deserves, and to fight it with the weapons the Lord Himself has put into the hands of those who believe."

The Rev. Msgr. Thomas J. Herron, S.S.L., S.T.D., pastor, St. Laurence Parish

"Many of our young people in Papua New Guinea feel that when they have sinned, they are victims of Satan, that they are caught up in a sinful habits and that there is no way out. *Unbound* gives the real answer that they need the power of Jesus to break free of their sinful habits. By prayer they can be led out of their addiction and brought to Jesus, who gives them freedom."

Bishop Anthony Burgess, diocese of Wewak, Papua New Guinea

D0187656

"Neal Lozano's book is an exceptionally fine practical guide showing us how to receive help and to go about helping people who need deliverance. This book is non-sensational and well-balanced. He does not give quick, simplistic answers but tells us how to enlist the person's own defenses through repentance and spiritual growth in a marvelous process of being freed from any demonic forces that oppress Christians. If you want to learn about the deliverance ministry, or are already involved and want to learn how to minister more effectively, be sure to add this book to your library."

Francis MacNutt, Ph.D., president,
Christian Healing Ministries

"One of the best books on deliverance. I found the book engaging, exciting, helpful, clarifying and, most important, written for the whole Church. This is a book every believer should read, and I believe it should be part of the training of every church's ministry team for altar work. It will equip you to minister to those who are being oppressed and, just as important, do so in a loving counseling environment."

Randy Clark, founder, Global Awakening

"Neal Lozano has been helping people for many years achieve levels of peace and freedom in their lives that they had never hoped to experience. I'm so glad Neal has taken the time to write this book and share this valuable wisdom with many others."

Ralph Martin, Renewal Ministries

"A breakthrough book that is much needed because many Christians today seem to dismiss the presence of evil spirits as something of another time and place, and fail to avail themselves of a ministry to which Jesus Christ Himself calls us—the ministry of healing. In his clearly written, biblically based book, the author reminds Christians that deliverance or liberation from evil spirits is a continuing and normal part of the Christian experience. When we learn to cooperate with God's grace, we are set free.

"Surveys on spirituality and faith, as well as my own personal experience in the healing ministry, lead me to be profoundly thankful that this book has been written. It will bring new life and hope to countless Americans trapped in emotional, physical or spiritual bondages, and will send a powerful message to the Christian community as a whole."

George Gallup Jr., chairman, The George H.
Gallup International Institute

"The most helpful book I know for dealing with evil spirits and related impairments in people's lives. It makes an enormous contribution in sharing the path to internal freedom through the process of renunciation. The reader will experience new hope in acquiring freedom in Jesus Christ."

The Rev. Michael Scanlan, T.O.R., chancellor,
Franciscan University of Steubenville, co-author,
Deliverance from Evil Spirits

"Those of us who have practiced deliverance and taught others to do so have learned to value books that provide basic instruction in this area, especially those based on a lot of effective experience. *Unbound* is such a book, and very usable as a basic introduction to a deliverance ministry. If you are looking for a good book to start with, I recommend this one."

Dr. Charles H. Kraft, School of World Mission,
Fuller Theological Seminary

"*Unbound* presents a practical, faith-filled way for Christians to rid their lives of the devil's influence, and sound advice for helping others experience deliverance from the work of evil spirits. It is a must-read for anyone who wants to enjoy the fullness of spiritual freedom that Jesus won for us by His death and resurrection."

Bert Ghezzi, author,
Voices of the Saints and *Mystics and Miracles*

UNBOUND

UNBOUND

A Practical Guide to Deliverance

NEAL LOZANO

Chosen
a division of Baker Publishing Group
Grand Rapids, Michigan

© 2003, 2010 by Neal Lozano

Published by Chosen Books
A division of Baker Publishing Group
P.O. Box 6287, Grand Rapids, MI 49516-6287
www.chosenbooks.com

New paperback edition published 2010

Printed in the United States of America

                    Library of Congress Cataloging-in-Publication Data
Lozano, Neal, 1949–
    Unbound : a practical guide to deliverance / Neal Lozano. — New pbk. ed.
       p.   cm.
    Originally published: c2003
    Includes bibliographical references (p.   ) and index.
    ISBN 978-0-8007-9412-5 (pbk.)
    1. Exorcism. I. Title.
    BV873.E8L69 2010
    235′.4—dc21   2010011233

Unless otherwise noted, all Scripture is taken from the Holy Bible, New International Version ®. NIV.® Copyright © 1973, 1978, 1984 by Biblica, Inc.™. Used by permission of Zondervan. All rights reserved worldwide. www.zondervan.com

Scripture marked NASB is taken from the New American Standard Bible ®, Copyright © 1960, 1962, 1963, 1968, 1971, 1972, 1973, 1975, 1977, 1995 by The Lockman Foundation. Used by permission.

Scripture marked NKJV is taken from the New King James Version. Copyright © 1979, 1980, 1982 by Thomas Nelson, Inc. Used by permission. All rights reserved.

Scripture marked RSV is taken from the Revised Standard Version of the Bible, copyright 1946, 1952, 1971 by the Division of Christian Education of the National Council of the Churches of Christ in the USA. Used by permission.

Note: Names have been changed throughout the manuscript to protect those whose stories appear here.

In keeping with biblical principles of creation stewardship, Baker Publishing Group advocates the responsible use of our natural resources. As a member of the Green Press Initiative, our company uses recycled paper when possible. The text paper of this book is comprised of 30% postconsumer waste.

10 11 12 13 14 15 16   7 6 5 4 3 2

Contents

Contents

Acknowledgments

For several years I struggled with the thought of writing a book on freedom from the influence of evil spirits. Having written before, I knew the kind of commitment and sacrifice it would take. I needed to know it was God's plan and not simply mine. Upon returning from a powerful mission trip, my wife, Janet, and I gathered in thanksgiving with our brothers and sisters in the House of God's Light Community, a Christian community located in Ardmore, Pennsylvania. As we finished prayer Ann Stevens, a longtime friend and member of the community, looked at me and said, "When are you going to write your book? I will help you!" It was one of those moments that stood still. As the minutes passed the words lingered. I knew God had spoken. It was His word to me, and I could rely on His help. I want to thank Ann for her help but most of all for speaking the words that released faith.

I want to thank my partner, my friend, my lovely wife, Janet, who stood by me with encouragement and support. Without her intercession, discernment and patience this book would not have been written. Thank you, Janet, for the sacrifice you have made and for your constant "yes" to those in need.

Janet was the chief of an army of editors and assistants I enlisted to rake over what I had written. Thank you, Ann Stevens, Jacqueline Harper, Rachel Bader, Kathy Pugh, Gosia Wojcik, Evelyn Bence and Angie Kiesling.

I want to thank Pablo Bottari for believing in me, for being an instrument of the Lord's compassion and wisdom. I want to thank Fr. Mike Scanlan for being a rock of godly wisdom in the area of deliverance and for his counsel through the years. I wish to thank Craig Hill for the wisdom he imparted to me about blessing through his "Curse to Blessing" seminar. I wish to thank all those who through their labor to set the captives free have gained and passed on wisdom that I have absorbed and no longer remember from where it came.

I wish to thank those who read the first draft, giving me such valuable input: Rev. Edward Crenshaw, Pastor Clifton Martin, Msgr. Thomas Herron, Rev. Michael Scanlan, Bert Ghezzi, Ben Dunning, Bill and Barbara Cassada, and finally Jane Campbell, the editor of Chosen Books.

I especially wish to thank all those people who trusted us with their secrets and allowed us to witness the work of the Lord in their lives. To those who allowed me to share their stories in this book may I say thank you; you have truly understood the gift of God. You have been blessed; now you are a blessing to others.

Foreword

Neal Lozano is careful to lay a foundation of love for and life in Jesus Christ as the requisite basis for all deliverances. His book *Unbound* sings of love in our Lord as the foundation of all ministry. We have seen many practitioners of deliverance who have not ministered out of the Lord's love and have unnecessarily frightened and wounded those they deliver. Lozano teaches that sensitivity and courtesy throughout deliverance sessions need to be written on the hearts of every deliverance minister.

Neal has the ability to write of high spiritual matters, which are sometimes complex, with engaging simplicity. This can move the field of deliverance out of exclusivity in ministry by a few "gifted" ones into the province of normal, everyday lay Christians. Our loving Lord has long wanted this. He wants Christians of all walks and levels of maturity to be able to deliver one another. Neal's book has already helped move us in that direction.

Tough cases will always remain, requiring expert ministry. For these, I hope lay Christians have the wisdom and common sense to refer to others what lies beyond their own calling and expertise.

The psalmist testifies, "My heart is not proud, nor my eyes haughty; nor do I involve myself in great matters, or in things too difficult for me" (Psalm 131:1, NASB). It is almost guaranteed that anyone who enters deliverance ministry will come up against cases, sooner or later, beyond his or her expertise. Pride and presumption can occur and cause the ministry to fail or the ministering one to get into trouble. There is always that risk when God's people are called into deliverance or other kinds of spiritual warfare.

But Jesus is Lord and able to rescue—and teach some hard lessons of wisdom in the process. I hope Neal's book can so call the Body of Christ into the work of deliverance that wisdom will guide with requisite restraint and caution, coupled with holy boldness.

Deliverance ministry calls for humility, and Neal Lozano's book is so replete with that welcome attitude that I, for one, believe it can call into deliverance ministry with minimum risk.

For that posture of humility, coupled with holy boldness, I heartily recommend that readers not only study this book but keep it handy as a reference for daily use, and spread its message to others, helping many needy people find Christians able to help.

To date, the fields are ripe to harvest—so many need deliverance—and there are too few laborers. May this book enlist an army.

John Loren Sandford
Co-founder, Elijah House Ministries, Inc.
Co-author, *Deliverance and Inner Healing*

Introduction

He has delivered us from the dominion of darkness and transferred us to the kingdom of his beloved Son, in whom we have
redemption, the forgiveness of sins.

Colossians 1:13–14, RSV

In January 1970, my life was changed forever when God revealed His love to me.[1] Shortly after, however, I began to notice
that the devil brought opposition to me when I was seeking to
serve the Lord. Whether it was an ill-timed sickness before a
retreat, or my back going out before I was scheduled to speak,
I became aware of how Satan used my fear to cause physical
symptoms in order to deter me. I began to understand that
temptation was not just a struggle against personal weaknesses but was in fact a strategic, demonic campaign to derail
me and to destroy my faith.

As I read the Scriptures, I noticed the many references to
the work of demons and to the freedom that Jesus brings
from evil spirits. I read whatever I could find on deliverance.
I listened intently to people's stories about being freed from
spiritual bondage in the name of Jesus. I became increasingly aware of a need for greater freedom in my life and the

lives of those around me. The only help I knew of, the only help I could offer other struggling Christians, were familiar Scripture verses I thought I understood: "Resist the devil and he will flee from you" (James 4:7, RSV); "Then you will know the truth, and the truth will set you free" (John 8:32). Yet something was still missing. I did not yet know how to practically live the truth of those verses.

About fifteen years later, the Lord taught me how to resist the devil and the ways the truth sets us free when a godly man, through the power of the Holy Spirit, delivered me from the influence of an evil spirit, a spirit that had kept me in real spiritual bondage rooted in a deep wound from my past. That event was hugely significant. I was able to take hold of the freedom Christ won for me in a new way. Over the years, I have been able to assist hundreds of others to do the same as my wife, Janet, and I have traveled the country and the world teaching at UNBOUND: Freedom in Christ conferences.

I believe in deliverance. Yet I also believe that most of our spiritual freedom comes when we learn the truth of who God is and we actually believe what He has said about Himself, about us, and about His workings in our lives. Trusting God, along with resisting temptation, repenting of sin, renouncing the works of the devil and forgiving those who have harmed us, accounts for ninety-eight per cent of our deliverance. Many of us, though, do not find complete freedom until we have gained that last two per cent: when we command the enemy to leave.

I teach this understanding of deliverance as the "Five Keys." These five prayer principles—repent, forgive, renounce in the name of Jesus, take authority in the name of Jesus, and receive the Father's blessing—are carefully explained and modeled in the chapters that follow. Each key addresses issues at the heart of our inability to take hold of the redemption that we have been given in Christ. Once deep heart issues are dealt with in this non-confrontational style of deliverance, freedom comes. It usually comes quietly. At one of our conferences in Kenya, the leaders expressed great relief at this. "You mean we do not have to shout and scream to help those in bondage?" We have heard similar comments in many other places, as Christian leaders have adopted the *Unbound* model.

The *Unbound* model of deliverance has been introduced and used around the world, in countries as far away as Ghana, Rwanda, and Papua New Guinea. To date, *Unbound* has been translated into Spanish, Ukrainian, Polish, Slovakian, and Slovenian. A Russian translation is in process.

A Christian friend of mine, a psychologist who does not believe in the devil, sent me the following anecdote after she read the first draft of this book.[2]

> Two boys were walking home from Sunday School after hearing a strong sermon on the devil.
>
> One asked, "What do you think about all that Satan stuff?"
>
> "You know how Santa Claus turned out," the friend replied. "It's probably just your dad."

I can understand her skepticism. I also appreciate the truth in the anecdote. The level of influence of evil spirits in one's life is often rooted in one's early experience or lack of experience with dad, mom, and the traumas of life. The Scriptures tell us, "Your enemy the devil prowls around like a roaring lion looking for someone to devour" (1 Peter 5:8). What better prey for the lion than one who has been wounded? As you will read, this book is not so much about evil spirits as it is about acknowledging the doors we have opened to their influence and learning how to close them. Deliverance is no more about the devil than the Exodus was about Pharaoh. Rather, deliverance from evil spirits removes obstacles so we may receive, in Christ, the Father's blessing.

In this book, I focus on spiritual freedom in the context of the normal Christian life. Many people have gone to counseling, confessed their sins, pursued a God-centered life and done all they know to be free from spiritual bondage in specific areas of their lives. No matter what they do, they find no relief. Many faithful, committed believers have lived with hidden sin, compulsion, and fear due to spiritual deception. It may never have occurred to them that they might need deliverance from evil spirits.

Before my wife delivered our first son, we went to a birthing class so we would understand the process and not be frightened by the unknown. Education taught us how to deal with our fears. I have written this book for the same reason: so that you will know how to cooperate with the Lord as He sets you free. It is written from the heart with a desire to speak to your heart and help you along the way. Yes, I hope this book will contribute something to the search for a balanced, safe, and faithful approach to the ministry of deliverance. But my primary interest is speaking to the hearts of those who seek deeper conversion to our Lord Jesus. Jesus is our liberator. He is the truth, and He has told us that the truth sets us free.

How to Read This Book

You are invited to take a personal journey through the first part of the book (chapters 1–9). Each chapter ends with a prayer and reflection designed to help you start a dialogue with the Lord. You may take this journey alone, or with a friend you trust, or in a small group with a trusted leader. My prayer is that you will encounter the Holy Spirit working in you to bring you to greater liberty.

Part 1 is a step-by-step reflection on the various principles that form the basis for prayer that leads to freedom and blessing. They are intended to help you make a faith response. You might read these chapters before and/or after someone prayed with you. The more you understand, the less control

18

the enemy has. Your understanding will help expel fear and reduce the likelihood of disruptive manifestations of evil spirits.

Chapters 1 through 9 cover these points:

- Because of Jesus, we have hope and can ask for the blessing we need.
- Jesus is our hope; He is our Savior.
- Jesus saves us from sin and from Satan's plan for our lives.
- Jesus reveals to us our hearts so that we can repent.
- Jesus gives us the power to forgive others and to renounce the enemy in our lives.
- We have authority over the devil's influence in our lives in the name of Jesus.
- God wants to bless us by revealing who we are, so we might fulfill our destiny.

I suggest that you journal, as you progress through the principles in this book. Keep a private record of the Lord's message to you and of your response, whether it is dramatic or a more gradual awareness of God's conviction, presence and power to transform and bless you.

The second part of the book focuses on how to assist others in the prayer for deliverance[3] and how to apply the principles in the first section. Part 2 will be helpful even for readers who rarely have the opportunity to pray for others.

Many people with pastoral responsibility use this book as a tool to prepare people to receive personal ministry. Asking people to prepare for ministry by reading the first half of the book provides an opportunity for deeper insight into issues that need to be addressed and a better understanding of how to cooperate with the process of liberation.

It is my deepest desire that those of you who have not received transformative help in the past or have not been understood by those trying to help you would receive hope through this book. As you look to the Lord to help you, continue in the basics: worship, prayer, repentance, fasting, discipline and spiritual counseling, and encountering the power of the Gospel, which sets the captive free. Deliverance is not a magic pill; it is part of the glorious ongoing work of the Holy Spirit transforming the lives of those who are being conformed into the likeness of the Son (Romans 8:29).

This book is about the hope and freedom that is ours through Jesus Christ. This freedom is released as we learn to cooperate with God's grace and gain the victory He has already given us.

> Long my imprisoned spirit lay,
> Fast bound in sin and nature's night . . .
> My chains fell off, my heart was free,
> I rose, went forth, and followed Thee.
>
> —Charles Wesley

When I first wrote *Unbound*, George Gallup called it a breakthrough book. Since then many others have said the same. It has been a vehicle for transformation in thousands of lives throughout the world. We regularly hear from people who have opened doors to freedom as they have read the chapters, personalized the message, and prayed the suggested prayers. The book has prepared others for an initial encounter with their Redeemer. Deliverance is the great theme of Scripture and the eternal purpose of Jesus Christ. It is the power of God destroying the works of the devil in our lives so we may receive the inheritance we have in Christ: the kingdom of God (see Colossians 1:13; 1 John 3:8).

PART 1

FREEDOM

1

Freedom to Hope

Jesus was savior. He rescued men from the evil and hopeless situation in which they found themselves; he broke the chains that bound them to the past and gave them a power which enabled them to meet the future.

William Barclay

"Good-bye. Thank you. Now I have hope!" Anna[1] had seen a lot by the age of nineteen. Her father traveled extensively, but even when he was home he was emotionally absent. Anna experienced torment and confusion growing up with her alcoholic mom and older brother. When she came to my wife, Janet, and me, sadness covered her. Evasive in her speech, she was unable to lift her head to look at us as she spoke. She had recently come to the Lighthouse Fellowship in Poland and had begun to pursue the Lord.

"Is there anyone you need to forgive?" we asked.

"Yes, but I'm afraid I will hurt the person if I tell you." A moment later she did name someone: "My mother drinks."

"Anna, if you want to be free, you need to let Jesus help you forgive," I told her. "Make the decision and say the words, and Jesus will do the rest. Do you want to?"

"Yes," she confessed.

Yet she could not repeat a short prayer after me. She couldn't speak. As I prayed for her and listened with my spirit, the Lord opened her heart to me, and I experienced the agony of her loneliness and desperation. "Lord," I prayed aloud, "Anna has lived in chaos and has never known what to expect. She wanted to fix things but couldn't." She began to sob. "But the thing she doesn't understand is why You didn't do anything. She knows You are God and can do anything. She has cried out to You; she has begged You; she has cried herself to sleep night after night, and You did not answer."

Now Anna was sobbing uncontrollably, wrenched with the pain of years of agony. Janet and the interpreter wept with her as God allowed them also to experience the depth of her pain. Then I prayed, "Lord, I don't understand. I don't understand why You didn't do something." We all wept together before the Lord.

"Now, Anna, would you renounce a spirit of unforgiveness, hurt and torment?" I asked her. "Will you say, 'I forgive you, Mom'?" She was ready, for she knew that others felt her pain. Most of all she knew her pain in a new way, as she allowed it to be brought to light.

"I forgive you, Mom, for your drinking and for rejecting me and for all the confusion and hurt. I forgive you for not loving me the way I needed to be loved." Then she renounced sadness, self-rejection, condemnation and self-accusation. She was being set free. We knew Anna had a long journey ahead, but we were grateful she was in a fellowship of believers who could help her as she continued to seek God's good plan and deny the devil access to her life.

The next day, her face was bright and her personality was joyful, not sad. We discovered her wonderful sense of humor. She brought her family to meet us. Before we left town she

24

waited by herself for more than an hour so she could get a picture of herself with us and say the words that still stir our hearts, "Thank you, now I have hope."

Desperate for Hope

Anna was an ordinary person in a very difficult and painful situation. Hopelessness and despair were slowly destroying her. While your situation may be very different from Anna's, is there an area of your life marked by hopelessness? Have you, like Anna, cried out to God day after day without a change? Has an attitude of resentment toward God crept into your heart and created a sense of distance when you try to approach Him? Is there something you have confessed over and over, but it has never changed?

For some people the need for hope is much more subtle, hidden. A longtime friend came to me for counsel because he struggled in several areas of his life. I asked Dave if he would like to renounce some of the areas he mentioned. He agreed. Here he tells his story:

"I prayed earnestly with Neal but sensed nothing out of the ordinary. Then Neal mentioned renouncing 'despair' and 'hopelessness.' Something happened. I found myself struggling to reject these spirits. As I tried, a well of emotions seemed to be attached to each, and I struggled to say them verbally without difficulty. As I did, anguish and pain rose up, and these emotions went with the rejection of the spirits. It was short, acute and real. A calming effect and a sense of relief followed this.

"A week or so after the prayer, I experienced a situation that in the past would have caused me great anguish and, yes, fleeting despair (although I would not have recognized it as despair or hopelessness). Although I reacted with concern, my emotions and thought patterns did not stoop to a lower, darker level. I believe that a door in my thought patterns and emotions that would have taken me down into a darker place has been shut. It isn't there now. It's up to me to keep that door shut."

It took me by surprise as well. I knew Dave as an enthusiastic Christian, always ready to serve and encourage others. Someone he greatly respected had betrayed him more than fifteen years earlier. He thought it had been resolved, yet in that situation a spirit of hopelessness, unidentified and hidden to Dave and to those around him, gained access and lingered in his life.

In some way Dave had grown resigned to his lack of hope. Maybe you feel hopeless in some area of your life, and you search for ways to numb the hopelessness. Some of us adjust our thinking to "It's just me; that's the way I am"; "It's something I will have to live with"; "It's not really that bad; I will get through."

Too Discouraged to Hope?

Prior to being set free a friend of mine struggled with overeating. She wrote: "I lately found myself sliding back down the slippery slope of eating when I wasn't hungry, which turned into being whenever I was angry, frustrated and/or alone. Yuck! Back came the few pounds I'd lost along with plenty of hopelessness, guilt, anger, depression. I was so frustrated, because I knew better, but was still being disobedient and feeling cut off from God; it was like I couldn't hear Him or approach Him until I got this food-obedience thing together. I guess you can imagine the guilt/condemnation package that comes with such thinking. Anyway, I've been stuck and struggling, to put it mildly. I'm just so tired of being overweight and out of control."

Can you relate to her dilemma? You could substitute any number of strongholds here: "I have this fear of rejection"; "I am a compulsive perfectionist"; "I am addicted to pornography"; "I have a fear of death"; "I have a fear of abandonment"; "I cannot forgive"; or "I have thoughts of suicide."

Of course, these things are not solely attributed to the work of evil spirits, but for many, the influence of evil spirits is the one area that has gone unnoticed and unaddressed in the pursuit of God's healing.

Proverbs 13:12 tells us that "hope deferred makes the heart sick, but a longing fulfilled is a tree of life." Hope is confident expectation for good; the ultimate good is heaven. The Scriptures say that Christ in us is that very hope, the hope of glory (Colossians 1:27). Does the power of the Gospel simply offer us in our bondage the hope of heaven? No. Colossians 1:13–14 says, "He has rescued us from the dominion of darkness and brought us into the kingdom of the Son he loves, in whom we have redemption, the forgiveness of sins." We have already been rescued (transferred, delivered) from one kingdom to another, yet full realization escapes us. I think of the children of Israel wandering in the wilderness. Through Moses, God had delivered them from the Egyptian taskmasters, and yet they held onto their slave mentality. A whole generation of Israelites died in the desert before the people were ready to cooperate with God, taking hold of the promises He had given them. Do you have a "slave mentality" that still needs to be defeated?

Too Disappointed to Seek Help?

Perhaps years ago you went through prayer for deliverance and it traumatized you so much that you never want to do it again. Maybe someone prayed for you and it was not successful, or those praying for you did not demonstrate love and respect when you were most vulnerable. Maybe you have a twisted idea about deliverance from evil spirits and get "weirded out" by the thought, "You mean, I might have a demon?"

Perhaps you have gone to your pastor or priest several times through the years. You have confessed your sins and received good advice—things to do, prayers to pray, encouragement to avoid evil and ways to discipline your thoughts and actions— yet your continued failure has increased your despair.

Perhaps you have been to counseling and it really helped. You now understand why you do the things you do, but the inner person has not changed. Maybe you have been to counseling for many years and very little has changed, so you no longer expect anything more than being able to cope.

You might be like many others, thinking about counseling, but because of financial restraints or pride, you never make that call for help. *I hope you make that call for help and talk to someone one more time.* We can all benefit from wise counselors who listen and understand.

Professionally trained counselors are a gift, an important resource, but there is only one Savior. It is unfortunate that pastors and church leaders feel so helpless, as if the Gospel has no power. Too many Christians are quickly turned over to professional counselors when problems surface. The power of the Gospel is much greater than that of a gifted counselor (although the two work together in a wonderful way). If counseling is needed, those in pastoral ministry need to know how to work together with the counselor to minister to the wounds of the soul.

A New Kingdom

"The time has come," [Jesus] said. "The kingdom of God is near. Repent and believe the good news!" (Mark 1:15). Mark's gospel records these as the first words Jesus spoke after His forty days in the desert. Jesus is the "new Moses," breaking the hold of Satan and leading us out from under his dominion. Jesus is the "new Joshua" leading us into the

Kingdom of God, where God Himself is the ruler and His laws are written on our hearts.

One day friends of John the Baptist asked Jesus, "Are you the one who was to come, or should we expect someone else?" In their presence Jesus cured many who had diseases, blindness and evil spirits. He answered, "Tell John what you have seen and heard" (see Luke 7:20–22). Those under oppression were experiencing the manifestation of the Kingdom of God. This is the Good News! The broken and oppressed, free from their bondage and sickness, were entering into the Kingdom.

In ancient times, when a king conquered a city, he sent out heralds to declare the good news: There is a new way of living; you now live under a new authority! Heralds declared the name of the new ruler and the great benefits that would come from living under his rule. Cooperating with this declaration was a matter of life and death.

The Good News is that Jesus Christ has become our King. He defeated Satan and canceled our debts. Our greatest deliverance comes from submitting to Him as our Savior. Now that we have chosen His rule and submitted to His Spirit, we no longer live under the rule of the old king. You are under a new authority; you live in a new kingdom. Liberation from the influence of evil spirits deepens as we respond to God's initiative of taking new territory in our lives.

The Blessing of the Kingdom

Freedom from the influence of evil spirits is not an end in itself. Receiving the full blessing God has given us in His Son and becoming His disciple is. Deliverance releases us from bondage into blessing. The Hebrew sense of blessing *(baruk)* is meant to empower someone to prosper, to succeed and to thrive. All blessing finds its source in God. After creating man and woman on the sixth day God blessed them and said to them, "Be fruitful and multiply, and fill the earth and subdue it; and have dominion . . ." (Genesis 1:28, RSV). To speak a blessing is to be God's instrument.

In biblical times a spoken blessing was meant to bring protection and help on a journey. It was meant to provide grace for life's journey. A blessing means to speak well of a person. It is the opposite of a curse. Awareness of God's blessing and our need to bless others was so deeply rooted in ancient Jewish culture that the word *shalom* is still used as a form of greeting. *Shalom* means peace, completeness, harmony, health and welfare. It is summarized in the godly plan identified in Jeremiah 29:11 (RSV): "For I know the plans I have for you, says the LORD, plans for welfare and not for evil, to give you a future and a hope." Here the word *shalom* is translated to the phrase "plans for welfare and not for evil."

This is what God intended for us from the beginning, and now in Christ we have indeed received every spiritual blessing (Ephesians 1:3). The fullness of what it means to be blessed is to know Christ and the truth of our identity and destiny in Him. It is to know that He has special plans for our future.

As we seek to receive the blessing of the Father, we can look to the example of how God spoke blessing into His Son, Jesus. Before starting His public ministry, Jesus came to John to be baptized. Knowing that Jesus did not need a baptism of repentance, John said, "I need to be baptized by you" (Matthew 3:14). But Jesus had come to earth to be one of us. Though divine, He identified with our sins. The sacrificial Lamb of God came to die so that He might redeem us and be our doorway to the mercy of God. Jesus' baptism is the first recorded act of His embracing His destiny as the saving Lamb of God. As Jesus came out of the water, the Spirit of God descended on Him, and a voice from heaven said, "This is my Son, whom I love; with him I am well pleased" (Matthew 3:17). God was declaring who Jesus was and His fatherly delight in Him. Entering our world of pain and suffering, Jesus brought with Him the favor of the Father, the

Father's blessing. Romans 5:10 says Jesus came to reconcile us to the Father. This blessing that Jesus received has been imparted to us. In Christ these words, this relationship, belongs to us. "How great is the love the Father has lavished on us, that we should be called children of God! And that is what we are!" (1 John 3:1).

Words of blessing affirm our identity and prepare us to fulfill our destiny. Each of us has a purpose, a contribution to make to the unfolding mystery of God's plan, something that will give praise and honor to the One who called us for all eternity.

> In him we were also chosen, having been predestined according to the plan of him who works out everything in conformity with the *purpose* of his will, in order that we, who were the first to hope in Christ, might be for the praise of his glory.
>
> Ephesians 1:11–12, emphasis added

Liberation from spiritual bondage frees us to receive the blessing God has given us in His Son so we might live for the praise of His glory. God is pleased when we seek all that He has for us in Christ.

Hope Enough to Ask

God wants us to ask to be blessed. I love the Old Testament story of Jacob, not because he lived a spotless life, but because he so desperately wanted to be blessed. He knew God had blessed his grandfather Abraham, and he conspired with his mother to inherit the birthright from his brother Esau through trickery. After doing so he ran away from home. Years later he knew he had to return and face Esau, and here Genesis records another desperate moment in Jacob's life. In a night of agony, finally facing the truth about himself, Jacob wrestled with God (who had taken the form of a man) till daybreak (see Genesis 32:24). Realizing He could not overpower Jacob, the Lord touched Jacob's hip and wrenched it. How strange to imagine that God could not overpower Jacob. What was it in Jacob that could not be defeated? Exhaustion must have reached every part of his mind and body, and his hip must have hurt badly, and yet he would not let go. Finally the man said, "Let me go, for it is daybreak." Jacob replied, "I will not let You go unless You bless me." Jacob would not quit. He had wrestled with God all night, he was wounded and he refused to let go until he got his blessing. No longer would he have to rely on his own resources to prosper; in his struggle he surrendered to God's plans for his welfare and his future. God did bless him, even changing his name to Israel and making his sons the fathers of the twelve Hebrew tribes.

Are you seeking God's blessing? Does it seem like you have struggled all night—or even all your life? Perhaps you have been through hard times. Your pain has been exposed; like Jacob, you are wounded and know you will never be the same again. Perhaps it is daybreak and you are about to let go. It's time to say one more time, "I will not let You go unless You bless me."

Maybe you are saying, "I want to be free. I want to know the blessings God has planned for me, but I don't have the strength of Jacob." Be assured that God wants to meet you and work with you where you are. He wants you to turn toward Him and ask.

In a later chapter I share the story of Mike, a 26-year-old on the fast track to success. One of God's prodigal sons, his spiritual journey back to God began with a simple request, planted by a faithful Christian friend. Sensing a bit of spiritual hunger in him, she said, "Why don't you just ask Jesus to come and get you?"

This is a good place to start. Just pray, "Jesus, come and get me." Say it often. Say it out loud or silently. You may say it with other words. "Jesus, if You are real, please show me." Or there's another simple request: "Help me, Lord." Help doesn't always come when and how we expect it. Anna did not think she would have to wait so long for an answer. Nor did she expect God to send someone halfway around the world to help her. You can be assured, though, that when you ask God hears, and His response is on the way (see Matthew 7:7).

You have to ask. No one else can ask for you. No journey to freedom takes place without the grace of God and the power of His Spirit working in you. Jesus died to save you and set you free. Freedom from the influence of evil spirits is a doorway to a deeper experience of the new life we have been given in Christ.

Read On . . .

In the next chapter we will look at the reality of our enemy, the devil, and how he wants to keep us from living out our destinies as children of God. In subsequent chapters of part 1, we will discuss five spiritual keys that free us from the bondage of evil. I use the key metaphor because of the dual purpose of keys, used both to lock and unlock doors.

Evil spirits gain influence in a life through doorways that are opened, often in childhood, by us or by other people. Through these doors Satan's lies and deceptions limit our access to the blessing of the Kingdom of God. By using the keys presented in this book, we can close the doors through which evil gains influence and at the same time open the doors through which Christ frees us and imparts blessing.

As you will see, this is not a once-in-a-lifetime grand opening—or closing. Rather, as we seek for and find new freedom, the Holy Spirit releases us from bondage at ever-deeper levels. God frees us and blesses us so that we may bless others. In part 2, I give instruction for how you can help someone else receive the gift of deliverance in Christ.

Wherever you are, just as you are, I suggest that you read on. Turning the page to chapter 2 is itself a hopeful effort. When Anna came to us she had few expectations. She came because we had prayed with a friend, and she thought she might as well give it a try. She left with hope and a new beginning. If you read on, you will have the same opportunity Anna had. You will learn how to stir up the gift of hope, to break with attachments to things that bind you and to release those who have wounded you. You will realize that the enemy's power has been broken and that you can cooperate with God's power as He reveals His special purpose for your life.

[Jesus said,] "So I say to you: Ask and it will be given to you; seek and you will find; knock and the door will be opened to you. For everyone who asks receives; he who seeks finds; and to him who knocks, the door will be opened."

Luke 11:9–10

Lord Jesus, come and get me. Capture my heart with Your love. I do not have the strength of Jacob; give me the courage to ask for the freedom and blessings that are mine in Christ. Use this book to renew my hope and expose those areas of my life that I have not surrendered to You. Show me who I am and Your plan for my life, my identity and my destiny. Bless me so that I may be a blessing to others.

2

Satan Has a Plan for Your Life

God's purpose is to crush our idols. . . . It is God himself
who takes us into his hands, God who—we think—attacks
us because he wants to remove that which is dearest to us and
to which we are unknowingly attached, heart and soul—the
little idol which we have carried with us for years and which
we adore as the true God.

Andre Louf

Raul's Release

Raul came with his wife to Janet and me for prayer. When
we asked him what he wanted prayer for, he replied, "My
pride; it has always been with me. I have always done well in
school and been popular. I married the homecoming queen.
I have been successful in business and pretty much whatever
I attempted. I have drawn my life from my own success."

Wow, I thought. *He understands how the spirit of pride
works. It will be a simple thing to help him repent, renounce
and be set free.*

"Shall we pray?" I asked.

"No, I have something else." He began to weep, uncharacteristic of a proud man. Truly he had been broken.

What could it be? I thought.

"Five years ago I had an affair," Raul told me. "I have confessed it many times. My wife has forgiven me, but I can't forgive myself. When I look at my wife and my children and feel the love and gratitude in my heart, what I did is always there. I think of how I betrayed them." He wept some more. This was a good man, committed to God and dedicated to Christian service.

What did I see in Raul? Through his success and giftedness, he had been tempted and later bound by a spirit of pride. And that pride had allowed him to hide from deeper fears and insecurities. Along with pride often come spirits such as superiority, arrogance, self-righteousness, self-justification and self-reliance, affecting a whole pattern of thinking. A person may learn to speak very humbly, but all the while he may be manipulating the way others perceive him. This was true with Raul. With pride leading the way, and self-centeredness, selfishness and arrogance following, many men follow a path that leads to adultery. Thoughts like, *I am not understood, I deserve it, I am not appreciated,* build on the underlying need to hide insecurity by remaining on top and in control. Now the very pride that led him to have an affair tormented him with accusations. *How could you do such a thing to your wife and family? You have failed in the only area of life that means anything.*

He tried to make up for his own sin by confession, remorse and self-accusation. His pride would not let him receive God's forgiveness and mercy. (Refusal to let go of guilt is often the work of pride, which deceives us into thinking we must redeem ourselves.) Self-justification required that he do something to make it better.

Raul's repentance had been completed long before we met. At this point, he needed to recognize and renounce the plan of destruction the devil had for his life. After we talked through the issues, he was ready for prayer: "In the name of Jesus, I renounce pride, self-righteousness, superiority. . . . In the name of Jesus, I renounce a spirit of adultery and unfaithfulness. . . . In the name of Jesus, I renounce a spirit of self-accusation and condemnation. . . . Is there anything else you want to renounce?"

"Yes, guilt."

"Anything else?" I asked.

"I don't think so."

"In the name of Jesus, I command every spirit that Raul has renounced to leave, now."

Raul felt new spiritual freedom. The influence of the evil one was broken, releasing him to new areas of Christian growth.

Years earlier Raul had been set up by an enemy intent on his destruction.

A Liar from the Beginning

Recently my wife and I watched the movie *Hook,* which tells the story of the grown-up Peter Pan. Peter now has children of his own and has forgotten his former life in Never Never Land. Captain Hook, seeking revenge, comes and steals Peter's children. Hook's plan is based on this scheme: the best way to get revenge on "the Pan" would be to win the affections of Pan's children and become a father to them. He wins the heart of Peter's son, Jack. He presents evil as good, distorts truth about his mom and dad, and brings suspicion on their motives. Gradually Jack begins to dress like the captain, and he forgets who he really is.

This story is an allegory for the human drama. Satan saw the dignity God gave to man and woman, created as they were in His image. Perhaps Satan even had a hint of mankind's destiny in Christ. In his hatred, Satan struck back at God by seeking to destroy His children. The cunning serpent-Satan recognized in Adam and Eve a potential to mistrust God's love, and he sought to capture their hearts and affections and become a father to them. Jesus referred to the devil as a father, the father of lies.

> You belong to your father, the devil, and you want to carry out your father's desire. He was a murderer from the beginning, not holding to the truth, for there is no truth in him. When he lies, he speaks his native language, for he is a liar and the father of lies.
>
> John 8:44

The word *devil* actually means accuser or slanderer.

By twisting God's words, questioning God's motives, making empty promises and presenting evil as good, Satan captured Adam and Eve, and they submitted to his rule. When God came into the garden to be with his children, they hid. "But the LORD God called to the man, 'Where are you?' He answered, 'I heard you in the garden, and I was afraid because I was naked; so I hid'" (Genesis 3:9–10).

Suddenly they were afraid of God and no longer received or perceived his love for them. They were also afraid of themselves, so they covered their bodies. That fear is in every person. Many of us deny it. We spend our lives trying to overcome it.

Afraid, self-absorbed, caring for themselves and not God, Adam and Eve began to act like the serpent, accusing each other, defending their actions and forgetting what God was really like. They believed the lie. They could no longer trust God with their lives. The serpent had stolen their hearts.

The enemy had succeeded; he misrepresented God and gained influence in the human race. He continues his influence through a host of evil spirits that seek to misrepresent God, deceive us and attach themselves to us. He often works through other people—those God intended to represent Him, such as parents and other caregivers. Those with the primary responsibility of presenting the character of God to the next generation are Satan's targets and prime agents.

God's children have been captured. God has a plan to win them back. He revealed Himself through Abraham as a Father, and He revealed Himself to a people who would prepare the way for the full revelation of His nature in Jesus Christ (see Hebrews 1:1–3), who came to earth and died sacrificially—then rose again—"to destroy the devil's work" (1 John 3:8) and reclaim us as God's children with a kingdom destiny.

In chapter 1, I described God's blessing of Jesus at His baptism. Note that immediately following that declaration of Christ's Sonship, Jesus "was led by the Spirit into the desert to be tempted by the devil" (Matthew 4:1). Why would God allow the devil to test His Son? Why would God allow the devil to tempt us? Let us return to the story of the Israelites in the wilderness: "Remember how the LORD your God led you all the way in the desert these forty years, to humble you and to test you in order to know what was in your heart, whether or not you would keep his commands" (Deuteronomy 8:2). The word *tempting* could be translated "testing" here. It was time for Jesus to know what was in His heart.

What did the temptations involve? At Jesus' weakest point—vulnerable from forty days of fasting—Satan said to Him, "If you are the Son of God, tell these stones to become bread" (Matthew 4:3). Satan's second temptation also began with, "If you are the Son of God" (Matthew 4:6). The third stated, "If you will bow down and worship me . . ." (Matthew 4:9). By testing Jesus' identity as God's Son, the devil tempted Jesus to act independently of the Father. He wanted Jesus to deny what God had declared about His beloved Son. Similarly, the trials in our lives, the challenges we face, are intended to reveal the truth that God has placed in our hearts. Satan may intend the trials for harm, but God's good plan intends them for good.

Bound by Lies

Though Satan's divisive plan—keeping us from the fullness of our destiny as sons and daughters of God in Christ—is different for each of us, depending on our unique situations and personalities, his plan for all of us is based on lies. Before I continue, let me also remind you of the words of Christ, the One who called Himself the Truth—and said "the truth will set you free" (John 8:32).

We have all internalized lies from the master of deception. These lies may serve as faulty foundations upon which we build our lives. Raul had built on self-reliance and from that core deception developed a system of thinking to protect the lie. This system of thinking is built the same way a bird builds a nest: one straw at a time. Likewise, the enemy brings us one damaging thought at a time. As a pattern of thinking is built based on the foundational lie, he finds a place to dwell and exerts greater influence on our emotions and will.

For example, a person like Raul may have embraced the Gospel and committed his life to Jesus. He knows with his mind that God loves him, and he may even have had a profound experience of God's love. But in the depths of his soul he cannot accept the love of God and the truth that through Jesus he is worthy of that love. The basic thinking remains: I have to be good enough to earn or deserve God's love. Does this sound at all familiar? Have you ever had trouble forgiving yourself as Raul did?

Second Corinthians 10:3 describes the conflict between truth and deception as a battle: "For though we live in the world, we do not wage war as the world does." The level of freedom we have surrendered to the enemy and the amount of influence he exerts is the most significant issue in the war. Scripture refers to these systems of thinking as strongholds. "The weapons we fight with are not the weapons of the world. On the contrary, they have divine power to demolish strongholds" (verse 4).

These strongholds block us from knowing the truth about God, His love and ourselves. They lead us to see many others as our enemies. Ephesians 6:12 says that our struggle is "not against flesh and blood, but against the rulers, against the authorities, against the powers of this dark world and against the spiritual forces of evil in the heavenly realms." Our real enemies are the powers of this dark world. Our thoughts deceive us.

Spiritual World

Unfortunately, many believers have lost the sense of interplay between the natural and spiritual worlds. The spiritual world has become something foreign. We may accept it intellectually, but practically it is not part of our Western worldview. For others it remains something weird that they would rather not think about. For those who have been awakened spiritually, confusion abounds.

Part of the problem is that the demonic world has been hidden. We do not understand it, and we tend to be afraid of that which we do not understand. Fear is one of the biggest obstacles in our cooperating with the Lord to set us free. The images of evil spirits lurking around us or inside of us trigger one of our most fundamental fears: There is something wrong with me that I cannot do anything about. Like Adam and Eve, our response is to hide.

Talk of evil spirits can bring up fears such as "Do I have a spirit?" We picture a foul little demon hiding in us in a secret place. Frightening! Gross! That is partially true, but the truth is the spirit is no fouler than the sin it hides behind. The sin we have accommodated, the thought pattern that offends the One who made us, the despair we carry and have grown used to, the lust we secretly feed, the unforgiveness and bitterness we nurse—these are the expressions of the influence of evil spirits. This is what they look like, but they don't look so bad to us because they are our demons. They are invited guests, our companions.

Some fear and confusion arises over the meaning of the scriptural word often translated as "possessed." A better translation of the Greek is "demonization." It actually means "to have a demon" or "to act under the control of a demon."[1] The English word *possessed* implies that one's life is under the control of the devil or a host of demons. It is a lot more serious than a demon exerting influence on an area or several areas of one's life. This is a good example of how the enemy wants to move us from a place of balance to extremes.

It is hard to consider that we may need deliverance from the influence of an evil spirit if we associate it with possession, especially as possession is displayed in the media. Many Christians allow for demonic activity in theory but think it has no practical consequence in the life of a believer. They believe demons can only influence those who do not know Christ. Can a Christian "have a demon," be under the influence of an evil spirit or have an area of life in which he or she has lost freedom? Yes. Most believers will admit that certain areas of their lives are not submitted to Christ. They are holding something back. In these areas the devil is still able to exert his influence and hold people in bondage.

Fueling our fear is the way movies and books often focus on extreme cases of bondage. Sickening manifestations of evil in response to the prayers of a priest or minister leave us wondering: Can Satan overtake a Christian's soul? Afraid of the devil and not secure in the love of Jesus, many are robbed of the authority they have in His name. The thought of being prayed over for deliverance brings to mind the demoniac Jesus dealt with in the gospel of Mark, chapter 5. The demoniac had superhuman strength to break chains. The demons spoke through the man and drove him insane, causing him to cut himself.

I believe powerful manifestations have more to do with the level of infiltration than the power of the demon, how much of the person's life and personality has been entwined with demonic presence. (Jesus indicates in Luke 11:26 that some demons are more wicked than others. Though demons carry different levels of strength, their power is insignificant compared to the power of the risen Lord.)

Over 95 percent of the people we have prayed for have no physical manifestations of evil. These things really do happen, but in my experience they occur in a minority of cases. Manifestations are found in the most severe cases. (Manifestations are more fully discussed in chapter 14.) They are also more prevalent in deliverance prayer models that emphasize confronting demons or when manifestations are expected.[2] Focusing on cases of violent manifestations keeps many from seeking deliverance, which I am sure does not bother the devil, who loves to remain hidden.

Hiding in the Trenches

The devil has many strategies. One is that he likes to hide in darkness, disguised, so he can deceive us from a secret place. Remember, to Adam and Eve he came disguised as a serpent, one of God's creatures.

Many times when we pray with someone we sense that the release from bondage moves from one chamber to the next. The person reveals one problem area and renounces spirits related to that problem, and then they see something deeper or darker—a door to another room. As they break free from an area of bondage, that which was hidden now becomes obvious.

A minister came to us asking for prayer. He confessed he had a fear of speaking in public. He also said he suffered from undue sexual temptation, but that he had managed to resist. Before praying with someone for deliverance, I ask a few questions—an informal interview—to get information about childhood dynamics and life patterns. "Tell me about your mom and dad," I asked.

"My mother was too busy for me," he said. "She was controlling and critical of my dad when he was not around. My dad was more honest. I played with my dad. He had to leave the country for a year to get work when I was seven. Our relationship was never the same after he returned."

As I listened to him and stayed sensitive to the Holy Spirit, I wrote down a number of things that could be renounced: fear, fear of public speaking, fear of rejection, fear of humiliation, fear of embarrassment, fear of criticism, insecurity, control, abandonment, rejection, hurt, loneliness and regret.

But what was the underlying issue? "Perhaps when your mom criticized your dad when he was not around, you felt insecure, wondering how she would speak about you when you were not around," I suggested.

"I never thought like that."

"Perhaps I am wrong," I replied, "but when we pray I would like to lead you in a prayer of forgiveness. If you identified with your dad and your mom criticized him, you may have felt as though you should do or say something, but there was nothing you could do or say. You may have taken it personally."

He looked at me with tears welling up and said, "Something is touching me."

We began to pray. "I forgive my mom for. . . ." Tears fell. Then we moved to his father. "I forgive you, Dad, for leaving me and not protecting me. . . ." Deep sobs rose as the man's unresolved pain was exposed. He had never considered how deeply he felt abandoned when his dad left for that year.

He renounced the list of possible related spirits and said, "I have peace." I thought it was over, but he said, "I have something else." The next chamber opened. He shared a couple of sexual encounters he had as a child—being part of a group of boys and girls that touched each other, and viewing pornography. More than twenty years later that same pornographic image would come to his mind. We prayed again. He spoke forgiveness to the boys who showed him the picture, and he renounced shame. Then he said, "There is one more thing. I have never told anyone about this in my life. When I was twelve a boy sat on top of me and tried to penetrate me orally. I was terrified as I fought my way out of the situation."

Once we renounced the spirits and commanded them to leave, great joy came upon my friend. The enemy had been exposed, light flooded the dark places and the old pattern of thinking was broken.

What was Satan's plan for this minister's life? I don't really know, but here are some of the pieces. God had called him to preach the Gospel. Fear of rejection had entered, and he found it hard to stand up in front of his peers and express the deep thing the Lord had done for him. I am sure it thrilled Satan to keep this man from moving in the authority God had given him, but Satan also had deeper plans. Working through hurt and self-doubt, Satan sought to lead him to discouragement and compromise. Now that root was exposed and the enemy's power (at least at a certain level) had been broken. My friend is free to walk in victory. He is no longer hiding in fear. He has the opportunity for his weakness to become his strength as he depends totally on God.

His trials developed in him a deep sense of compassion and sensitivity to the Holy Spirit. Being set free seemed to release a deeper sense of God's mercy. His fear of the devil lost its power. As he joined us in praying for others, it seemed evident to me that he has a special gift for speaking to the heart of those he ministers to. I believe he will grow in the gift of discernment by which many captives will be set free.

Seeking Attention

It may seem contradictory, but a second tactic Satan uses is to get attention, taking away from God what belongs to

God. One of the devil's temptations of Jesus was, "All this I will give you . . . *if you will bow down and worship me*" (Matthew 4:9, emphasis added). The deceiver continues to repeat this lie to us.

There is profound truth in these few sentences by C. S. Lewis: "There are two equal and opposite errors into which our race can fall about devils. One is to disbelieve in their existence. The other is to believe, and to feel an excessive and unhealthy interest in them. They themselves are equally pleased with both errors."[3] It is hard to maintain a healthy balance. It is as if the devil himself pushes us toward one of the two extremes.

Before a soldier goes to war, he is taught to focus on the enemy and his strategies. He learns how to defeat the enemy. Yet the soldier is not taught to look into the face of the person he is about to kill, wound or capture, or think about who the person is. He does not ask, "What is their life all about? How many children will they leave behind? How will the world be affected by the fact that they will no longer exist?"

Think of evil spirits as an enemy. It is tempting to become preoccupied with them. In Ephesians 6:11 we are directed to take our stand "against the devil's schemes." When I assist others in getting free from evil spirits, I focus on the individual and seek to understand the strategies of the enemy. What is his plan? What is the foundational lie? What areas of the person's life are being held in bondage? It is a mistake to dwell on how strong a demon is. This draws our attention away from the Lord. Demons are powerless in the lives of Christians when their right of entry is taken away. *When we realize this we will find ourselves thinking much less about demons and more about their schemes (tactics).*

Common Entry Points

As I pray with people for deliverance, I ask the Lord to show me the entryway, the faulty foundations, the lies on which the person has based their thinking. I encourage you to ask God for yourself: "Lord, show me the places where evil spirits have gained access to my life." Exposing the entry points sheds light on what is hidden in darkness, the place demons hide.

Following are some of the most common points of entry.

Response to trauma

In my experience the most prominent entryway is our response to trauma, abuse, family and friends. When a person experiences trauma or hurt, he or she searches for a way to deal with it, a way to protect self and be safe. Whether it is denial, fear, hatred, shame or a host of other responses, evil spirits want to exploit us through those responses, to exert influence and hold us captive.

The things buried in darkness have the greatest influence on us: the things we have never told anyone, the things we have not processed in light of God's love for us.

"When I was nine, I was raped by my friend who was fourteen," a young woman told me. "I have never told anyone what happened." My heart broke as I identified with the pain she had carried for the past eight years. The amazing thing was that she told me in a crowded room as we prayed for people following a talk on forgiveness. Up to that point, nobody had held out to her the hope of freedom from her torment. You can imagine Satan's schemes to limit her freedom: plans to keep things hidden in darkness, plans to sabotage her sexual identity and her relationships with men. This was the faulty foundation on which her thoughts had built since childhood.

The way we learn to cope with pain in our life, apart from the love of God, is a door to the influence of evil spirits. Just as God uses people as instruments of His love and mercy, Satan wants to use people as his instruments of rejection and condemnation. Natasha, a beautiful young woman from the Ukraine, had some trouble with rejection from her peers when she was small. When she was fifteen she fell in love for the first time. In her broken English she said, "He was my first big love." She had invited this older boy to be her escort at her sister's wedding. At the reception the boy had a heart attack and fell to the floor. For several hours she stood and watched as people tried to help, then she watched him die. She had heard about the seminar we were doing and said God told her in a dream that she would be set free. We found her to be a private and shy person, yet very talented. At 29, she had trouble entering into relationships and found it hard to get along in groups.

What was Satan's plan for her life? It began with a spirit of rejection. With rejection often comes a fear of rejection and self-rejection. This began when she was young and solidified in the trauma that brought such fear into her life. Patterns of isolation, shyness, loneliness and hopelessness developed, along with a fear of vulnerability combined with stubbornness and self-will. As we helped her identify these patterns that were closing her off, keeping her from freedom, we made no judgment as to whether they were spirits and, if they were, whether they were in her or simply tempting her. We led her through the keys to freedom—repenting, forgiving, renouncing—and I commanded every spirit she renounced to leave. Her response was, "I am free."

The next night she got up and admitted that though she "never speaks in front of groups," she wanted to tell everyone her story. Natasha had become so identified with her rejection it was a part of her personality, part of everything she did. She desperately sought the Lord to set her free from her torment. She came ready to renounce her old patterns of self-protection. The enemy's hold on her was broken. A year later we received a letter from her that ended, "It is true. I am free."

Involvement in the occult

A second common entryway is involvement in the occult. One young woman told us, "When I was thirteen I went to a

48

witch to read my fortune. She told me I would lose my first baby and have a car accident when I was 27. It was just a game. I did not think much of it. But as I grew and thought about marriage, I developed this fear of losing my first child. I am 19 and still do not have a driver's license. When I drive with someone I often have this compulsion to grab the wheel and turn the car into a tree."

In this situation the spiritual bondage came quickly because of the invitation she made to demons by going to a fortuneteller.

At one of our seminars we invited an impressive young medical student to be with us as we prayed for people. We wanted to help him learn how to pray for others. After the session he asked if he could receive prayer. When he was young his mother had taken him to a psychic healer. During the prayer he renounced the connection and any spirit that had come to him through the contact. He felt something lift and go. Later, he testified that it was as though he was under a cloud all his life and had never known it. Now the cloud was gone.

Another woman told us she thought there was a curse on her family. As she shared, I considered that it might not be a curse but simply a difficult marriage. I asked her to repent, forgive and renounce a number of things, and as soon as I spoke the word of command, she looked up as if she had just realized something for the first time: "When we bought our house it was owned by a witch. She had cursed all of our neighbors. When we moved in we found bones in our basement." What was hidden was uncovered. After prayer she left, declaring she was released from the bondage.

Self-inflicted curses

A third entryway is self-inflicted curses or pacts with the devil.

"I've been hearing voices for several years. Can you help me?" a woman asked me.

I asked more questions. "When did you start hearing them? What happened around that time?"

"When I was fifteen my mother was very sick," she said. "I had prayed that God would heal her. One night I was so angry with God that I turned from Him. I turned to the devil and made a pact with him. It was some time after that that I started hearing voices."

After a brief prayer the voices stopped. She recognized the entryway. It was very simple.

Circumstances of birth

It is quite common for children who have been adopted or children of divorce to benefit from prayer to be set free from spirits of rejection and abandonment. The following is a story of an unusual birth shared by adoptive parents.

In early January 1999, John and Sheila went to a seminar by Craig Hill called "From Curse to Blessing." They learned about God's desire to bless them and how to remove the obstacles that kept them from their blessing. As she sat in the seminar and leafed through the outline, Sheila came upon a list of sins that could break the continuity of blessings.

"What stood out on that list for me was 'conception out of wedlock,'" she told me. "I knew in that instant why we were there. Three of our children were adopted, and one in particular had an ongoing pattern of sin in his life. But then, as only the Lord can do, I was probed more deeply and realized that our first child's conception before we were married had consequences in his life as well. Though he appeared to have a good life, he, too, labored under an absence of blessing. We had confessed our sin long ago, but there never seemed to be any way to undo the harm caused by our sin."

In the context of the seminar John and Sheila readdressed their sin, and then later confessed it before their small group. "I think it was the first time I was genuinely sorry without any attempt at justifying our actions," Sheila said. "The next step we took we had never done before. We asked the Lord to go through our son's life and pour out blessings in all the places and times that blessing was withheld because of our sin."

This particular son and his wife had been married for eight years and were unable to conceive a child. They had tried fertility drugs with no success. They adopted a child from Russia in 1998. In March of 1999, three months after the seminar, their son called to say his wife had conceived a child without the help of any medical intervention. "This is our miracle baby," he said.

"You don't know just how much of a miracle this baby is," his parents told him.

"We shared with him our experience, and he was deeply touched when he realized that they had conceived within days of the seminar," Sheila said. "Sharing our story and our prayer together was another part of the healing that God had prepared for our son."

Associations and environment

Another entryway is the atmosphere in which we live. Have you ever heard the saying "Tell me who your friends are, and I will tell you who you are"? It carries a lot of truth. We tend to talk and act like those around us. Our surroundings and the environment we create affect us. When we begin to act or think like those we live with, we open ourselves to blessings that come with virtue or oppression that comes with rebellion and sin. This is illustrated in the book of Proverbs. "Do not make friends with a hot-tempered man, do not associate with one easily angered, or you may learn his ways and get yourself ensnared" (Proverbs 22:24–25). The open door may be the friends we choose, the forms of entertainment we indulge in or the area of sin to which we surrender our thoughts.

Willful sins

Repeated, willful sin is an open door to the enemy. Sins born out of lust can lead to the bondage of sexual addiction. Repetitious sins of deception can leave a person a compulsive liar or thief. Compulsive sin may indicate a need for deliverance from evil spirits. When a person is in spiritual bondage to sin, there is usually a deeper foundational entryway as well. A history of isolation and rejection or an early disconnection from one or both parents may be the foundation upon which an addiction rests.

Family sin

The family system in which we were raised may have fostered in us a vulnerability to the influence of evil spirits. For example, if raised in an atmosphere of anger and violence we would likely learn to respond to the frustrations of life with anger and violence. This learned pattern might become demonically empowered. Family bondage may be traced back generations (see Exodus 20:5–6; Deuteronomy 30:19). The cycle is ended when the evil spirits' power is broken and new patterns of thinking and acting are established.

This is illustrated in Cindy's story. Now in her twenties, Cindy grew up in a home of suppressed emotions. Marital problems left her parents emotionally and physically separated from one another. She never saw her parents express love to one another, she never saw either of her parents cry and she never saw them fight or argue.

As Cindy grew up, her mother encouraged her to be open and express her emotions. Her mom recognized the need for such expression, though she was incapable of it herself. Through Cindy's attempts to express emotion she realized the only accessible emotion was anger. But she was confused because she had no example of how to express any emotion appropriately, even anger. Whenever she did express emotion she felt guilty and over-apologized. Like her mother, Cindy could only appreciate emotions cerebrally.

She identified herself as rational and even-keeled; her friends commented that she was not an emotional person. But deep down something else was speaking, something hidden but always present: "Something's wrong with me; I don't have feelings."

Cindy was afraid to be emotional. She compensated for her emotional shortfall by maintaining a schedule full of activities. Her many accomplishments allowed her to experience success and thereby gain a sense of worth. The many acclamations were enough to hide her emotional disability from others, but not from herself.

Cindy asked us to pray with her for liberation. The first session dealt with some forgiveness issues. She renounced spirits of pride, control and perfection. It was a good experience, and she felt freer. A deeper work, however, was just beginning. Several months later, on a retreat, she said she wanted to be free from perfectionism and the fear of being out of control. As she stepped forward for prayer, she started to shake as though chilled to the bone (the room was warm). The shaking frightened her because she felt a loss of control, but she knew God had broken in and was touching her. She realized in that moment how much she had suppressed her emotions; they had been frozen.

We asked Cindy to renounce several things: perfectionism, fear of emotions and finally confusion. When she renounced confusion she immediately stopped shaking and sensed the refreshing of the Holy Spirit.

As Cindy learns a new way of living and has a family of her own, her freedom will become a source of blessing to her children and the generations to follow. If she did not courageously seek freedom from this pattern and the spirits associated with it, she would very likely have passed it on as a curse to the next generation.

Cooperation and Conversion

Yes, Satan has a plan for your life, but he needs your cooperation for it to succeed. God also has a plan for your life. Don't you long to see it fulfilled? If we have built our lives on the foundation of a lie, we need Jesus (the Truth) to expose that lie. In the next four chapters, I will share with you how to cooperate with the Holy Spirit to close the entryways and be set free from the influence of the evil one.

Ever deepening conversion is the process by which the structures of our thinking are exposed and we open the door to the One who gives us a new life. That new life continues to bring us to deeper conversion. It turns us from the power of Satan to the power of God (Acts 26:18), from the plan that Satan has for our life to the plan God has established before the foundations of the earth (Ephesians 1:11).

As you read on, I encourage you to remember major points of this chapter: First, that there is no reason to focus on a demon. An evil spirit is nothing compared to Jesus. The only power an evil spirit has is what has been given to him by us or by our parents or those who had responsibility for us when we were young. God has a plan for our lives. Therefore, whatever opposition a believer faces ultimately serves God's predetermined plan to conform us to "the likeness of his Son" (Romans 8:28–29) and advance the Gospel (see Philippians 1:12). Once the entryway is exposed, taking authority is very simple. The issue is not the evil spirit, his strength or his name; it is simply the lie, the entryway and the power of the name of Jesus.

Second, keep your eyes fixed on Jesus, the deliverer. Just as there is no reason to focus on a demon, there is no reason to become introspective, making an idol of your feelings. Ask the Holy Spirit to help you take control of your thoughts. "We demolish arguments and every pretension that sets itself up against the knowledge of God, and we take captive every thought to make it obedient to Christ" (2 Corinthians 10:5).

We take thoughts captive by following the instructions of Philippians 4:8: "Finally, brothers, whatever is true, whatever is noble, whatever is right, whatever is pure, whatever is lovely, whatever is admirable—if anything is excellent or praiseworthy—think about such things." We are strengthened also by praying, attending worship, hearing the Word, receiving the sacraments, meditating on Scripture and filling our minds with the truth. How else do we take our thoughts captive? By exercising the authority we have been given to break the power of evil spirits behind the thoughts that have held us captive.

Take a few minutes to ask God to show you what Satan's plan is for your life. Is there a faulty foundation stone of rejection, fear or another pattern of response to early trauma upon which you have built your thinking?

> This is the message we have heard from him and declare to you: God is light; in him there is no darkness at all. If we claim to have fellowship with him yet walk in the darkness, we lie and do not live by the truth. But if we walk in the light, as he is in the light, we have fellowship with one another, and the blood of Jesus, his Son, purifies us from all sin.
>
> *1 John 1:5–7*

I love You, Lord. Come bring Your light and expel the darkness. Bring Your truth and expose the lies. There are many things in me that keep me from giving and receiving love. Cleanse me by Your blood. Set me free from those lies that keep me from knowing Your love. I want to walk in the light on the path You have chosen for me.

As you read the next chapter, ask the Lord to show you the hidden things in your life and to give you the gift of repentance.

3

I Repent, I Believe

Only those who thus continue in their conversion truly know God. For they know their sin. Though they are confronted by the wrath of God, at the same time they discern the greatness and superior strength of God's love. They never cease to acknowledge their sin, in order in that way to proclaim God's mercy.

Andre Louf

In these next five chapters I want to place in your hands five keys. Picture a locked door. Opening that door represents liberation from spiritual bondage. This door has five locks, each requiring a key. As a believer in Christ, you have all the keys you need to be free from the influence of evil spirits. If one key has not been used the bolt remains in place and the door will not move. It may be nice knowing that you have used four keys, but it will not get you through the door to liberation. I present them in the order they are most commonly used, but they don't have to be used in this order. As I take you through an examination of these five keys, consider if there is one or several that you have not used properly. As

you do, meditate on the words of Jesus: *"Here I am! I stand
at the door and knock. If anyone hears my voice and opens
the door, I will come in and eat with him, and he with me"*
(Revelation 3:20).

Five Keys

1. Repentance and faith
2. Forgiveness
3. Renouncing the work of your enemies
4. Standing in the authority you have in Christ
5. Receiving God's blessing of your identity and destiny

These keys will open to you the abundant life promised
by Christ and close the entryways through which evil spirits
gain access to your life.

A Prodigal Son's Return

In chapter 1, I briefly mentioned Mike, a 26-year-old on
the fast track of success, advancing quickly in a telecom-
munications company. One day he found himself cornered
at a lunch reunion with Betsy, a former co-worker who
was visiting from out of town. Mike, a Catholic, had great
respect for her integrity and how she lived her Christian
commitment as a Baptist. As a co-worker she had taken an
interest in Mike, talking with him about the Lord. Betsy was
very direct. Before they ordered lunch, she looked straight
at him with her deep brown eyes. "How are you and Jesus
doing?" she asked. Mike generally thought he was doing
great. He had money, influence and personality. Everyone
liked him, except those who got in his way. But this question
probed deeper. Mike wasn't doing too well with Jesus. The
question exposed his world of alcohol, drugs and pleasure-
seeking.

"I'm not doing too well," he responded honestly, with a sudden sense of spiritual hunger. "If I had your faith I would be a good Catholic. I would be a very good Catholic." About ten years earlier Mike had vowed he would not be a hypocrite. If he was living a life that did not reflect his faith, he would not go to church. But now as he listened to Betsy, he confronted the most basic question: *Do I really believe in Jesus? If I do, how can I trust that this is not just an empty promise, a dead end?* Maybe he'd give the Christian life a try, but where to start?

"Okay. You got me," he said to Betsy. "What can I do?"

"Why don't you just ask Jesus to come and get you?" she said, sensing that a more complicated response would overwhelm him.

Mike could take that first step. With sincerity he repeated, "Jesus, come and get me!"

"Now what?" he asked Betsy.

"Do you have a Bible? Read your Bible every night as if it were God's word to you and Jesus is who He says He is. You might start with John's gospel," Betsy challenged him.

"Okay, is that it?" Mike wanted to know.

"Keep asking Jesus to come and get you, and go back to church."

Mike found the unread Bible his grandfather had given him for his confirmation. Each night he read and in the morning he got out of bed and immediately went to his knees. "Come and get me, Jesus," he prayed, followed quickly by, "In the name of the Father and of the Son and of the Holy Spirit, Amen." Two months later on a Wednesday evening, he sensed an inner voice urging, "Go to church."

Now I'm hearing voices, he chuckled to himself as he cranked up the rock music on his car radio.

"Go to church." This time it sounded like a command; he could not ignore it. Turning his car in the direction of a local church, he reasoned it couldn't hurt, for who would be at a Catholic church on a Wednesday night?

In the church Mike was surprised to find seventy people in the front pews. He sat down alone in the back. At that moment the priest came out to apologize for being late; his car had broken down. It was as if God had delayed the meeting, waiting for Mike to arrive. The priest explained that they were there for the fifth week of the Life in the Spirit Seminar. They were going to pray for the filling of the Holy Spirit for those who wanted to receive Jesus as their Lord. Knowing he wasn't part of the program, Mike stood up to leave. As he rose, he heard the priest say, "Can you hear me in the back? If you came closer I wouldn't have to speak so loudly." Now he was stuck.

A few minutes later Father John diverted from his planned script. "I see a few faces that are new to the group, and the Lord put on my heart that at least one of the newcomers has really been crying out to God, and in effect saying, 'Jesus, come and get me.'" Panic gripped Mike as he realized what this meant: God had sent him here. Something was going to happen to have a dramatic impact on his life; this was his time. Now he listened intently.

When it came time to make a public act of surrender to the Lord, Mike stepped forward. "Repeat after me," the priest said. "Do you renounce Satan?"

"I do." In that moment he knew the reality of evil in his life; he became aware that the devil is real and that these were not empty words.

"All his false promises?"

"I do." He saw the failures and emptiness of his life of sin.

"And all his works?"

"I do!"

"Do you believe in God the Father, Jesus His Son and the Holy Spirit?"

"I do."

Mike publicly declared the faith that he had been redis-
covering over the last few months. As the priest prayed with
Mike, he met the Holy Spirit with dramatic power.

During the mass that followed, he received the gift of repentance. Deep sorrow and remorse gripped him as he repented
deeply for his years of rebellion. He was humbled by the
recognition that God had reached out to him and brought
him to church that night so he could know his Lord.

The Prodigal and Repentance

In His Luke 15 parable of the prodigal son, Jesus revealed the
character of God in the father and something about each of
us in the two sons. First, let's look at the younger son's story.
The younger brother exemplifies people doing what they
want even though they know they shouldn't. We do them in
a spirit of rebellion and independence, or perhaps we simply
declare, "They are not so bad," or "That's the way I am,"
or "I'm doing everything else right—it is just this one thing;
I'm going to do it anyway."

The biblical story starts with a young impetuous son asking for his inheritance and leaving his father's house. He
travels to a far country where he foolishly spends the money
until he comes to his senses—a broken man—and decides
to return home.

> "How many of my father's hired men have food to spare,
> and here I am starving to death! I will set out and go back
> to my father and say to him: Father, I have sinned against
> heaven and against you. I am no longer worthy to be called
> your son; make me like one of your hired men."
>
> verses 17–19

He walks to his father's house and is surprised to see that
his father is out watching for his return. With great repentance, he falls into his father's arms, seeking pardon. How

does the father respond? He hosts a party. "'For this son of mine was dead and is alive again; he was lost and is found.' So they began to celebrate" (15:24).

The younger brother realized the wrong he had done, humbled himself and returned. This is a picture of true repentance: turning away from sin and turning toward God. It is like walking in one direction and then moving in a completely new direction. It is renewing one's mind, as the prodigal did, repeating to himself, "I will set out and go back to my father and say to him: 'Father, I have sinned against heaven and against you. I am no longer worthy to be called your son; make me like one of your hired men'" (verses 18–19). He turned away from his pride and rebellion and headed home. The process of repentance is completed in the restoration of relationship, the expression of the Father's affection and the receiving of the Father's blessing.

Great healing results when we repent, turn to God, and experience His love and acceptance, discovering who we really are through the revelation of who He is.

Personal Knowledge of Our Sin and Our Savior

All healing involves forgiveness. It begins with the incredible and immeasurable gift of God in the forgiveness of our sins through the death of sinless Jesus—God in human form. How deadly is our sin? How serious our offense? Consider the price paid to set you free: God the Father gave us His only begotten Son to become one of us, and to suffer and die for us on the cross. Our sins are a participation in sin, the collective rebellion of humanity against God that entered the human race in the rebelling of our first parents.

Some people who consider themselves Christians have never clearly understood and personally accepted the reality of who Jesus is as Savior. Going to church can seem empty if we lack a personal knowledge of sin and a relationship with the One who saves us.

I know many people who grew up in the church and accept the teachings of the faith. But a personal relationship with the Lord requires a time of conversion, facing not just the fact that we all sin but that I sin and my sinfulness requires a personal need for the Savior. When you consider His death and resurrection, do you take it personally—He died and rose *for your* liberation? Or is it simply a sign of His love for all humanity? Does your hope of eternal life rest completely on what He has done for you?

If you have tried to follow Christ and question whether you know Him as your Savior, I suggest you start with this prayer: "Jesus, show me what is wrong with me." It won't be long before you know your need for the Savior. As Betsy suggested to Mike, read the Bible as God's word to you and go to church. If you don't know Him in a personal way, seek out someone who does. Accepting the saving work of Christ is foundational to receiving the power to break the influence of evil spirits.

As we continue our Christian walk, we need to remain aware of that need for and reliance on Christ as Savior. Through ongoing conversion and dependence on the Savior, we can be kept out of the trap of religiosity. We do not have to end up like those "having a form of godliness but denying its power" (2 Timothy 3:5). A good definition of conversion is "accepting by a personal decision the saving sovereignty of Christ and becoming his disciple."[1] Conversion (or disciple-ship) is daily acceptance of the Savior and ongoing life as His disciple. Colossians 2:6 reminds us, "Just as you received Christ Jesus as Lord, continue to live in him."

Consider the Older Brother

Twenty years ago, I browsed in a Christian bookstore for something that would help me identify the sins in my life so

I could make a better confession. The major sins I carried into my Christian life had been dealt with. The list I used to pick from no longer applied. I didn't find a book that day, but I do believe God placed on my heart a desire to understand the hidden sins of the heart that would be fulfilled years later when I wrote my first book, *The Older Brother Returns*.

The title refers to the older brother in the parable of the prodigal son. He is mentioned at the end of Luke 15. The father meets the younger son with joy and asks servants to rustle up a party. The older brother comes in from the field and asks what's going on. Hearing the news of acceptance, the older brother refuses to attend the party, which prompts a conversation between him and his father: "All these years I've been slaving for you and never disobeyed your orders. Yet you never gave me even a young goat so I could celebrate with my friends. But when this son of yours who has squandered your property with prostitutes comes home, you kill the fattened calf for him!"

"My son," the father said, "you are always with me, and everything I have is yours."

My zeal to write the book came from an image of the prodigal returning to the father's house and meeting the older brother instead. What would have happened? Would he have ever made it home to his father? What would happen today if the prodigals came home and met the older brother in us? The lessons in my book on the older brother came from searching for answers through some very challenging times. The Christian community I led at the time underwent a painful splintering of relationships. A visitation of God that came in the form of judgment exposed our hearts and broke our pride. It was only then that I began to see the meaning of the older brother in the parable.

For years I simply pictured myself as the prodigal come home. I never forgot that moment when God revealed His love to me. As time went on I realized something was missing. My heart had grown cold. I did not realize I had become more like the older brother. The older brother looks good on the outside, but something is wrong on the inside. He does the right thing but for the wrong motives.

It reminds me of the Old Testament story of Samuel, whom God sent to the house of Jesse to anoint one of Jesse's sons as king. Samuel was impressed with Jesse's older sons, but the Lord said, "Do not consider his appearance or his height, for I have rejected him. The LORD does not look at the things man looks at. Man looks at the outward appearance, but the LORD looks at the heart" (1 Samuel 16:7).

In the case of David, God's chosen son, "looking at the heart" is good news. In the case of the older brother, it is bad news. It is bad news because we are often the last to know what is buried in our hearts. Jeremiah 17:9 says it this way: "The heart is deceitful above all things and beyond cure. Who can understand it?" Our own hearts can deceive us, but the Lord is not deceived. "The LORD searches every heart and understands every motive behind the thoughts. . ." (1 Chronicles 28:9).

The Sins of the Older Brother's Heart

Following are some sins of the heart that I've identified in the lives of Christians who've remained faithful to God in "outward appearance." Use this list to examine yourself for sins of the heart.

Legalism and self-righteousness

Legalism is our effort to find acceptance with God or others on the basis of our conformity to a set of rules, practices or teachings. We try to fit in based on our own effort. Self-righteousness is very similar to legalism. We think we deserve something because "we have slaved for him all these years." When someone we judge as being less worthy than us gets favored treatment, we say, "It is not fair."

Pride

Pride seeks to place us in control, to resist our dependency on God. We would rather be in control than be intimate. We pretend to be better than we are. We act religious and holy, but we know that what is going on inside is a different story. The older brother detests weakness and boasts of strength. Brokenness and desperation are not valued, but looking good and success are. In Matthew 5, Jesus tells us that the poor in spirit, those who mourn, and those who are hungry and thirsty are blessed. The older brother thinks he is never supposed to be weak.

Judgments

The older brother stands in a superior position of judgment toward others. We are told in the Scriptures not to judge (this refers to unrighteous judgments, not instances of discernment or recognizing right from wrong, good from evil). We can lock someone up in a prison by thinking, "That is the way they are they will never change." By labeling others we give ourselves a reason to withdraw from the relationship. The prison walls we build are really built to protect ourselves.

Fear

The older brother is afraid; he is not secure in his relationship with God. He doesn't understand that his relationship is based not on what he does but on God's love. Fear is the root cause for us to need to be in control.

Self-pity

We want people's compassion and sympathy more than we want to be free, more than we want to move on and place our trials behind us. If we let go of our self-pity we have to face that we are responsible for our own lives.

Bitterness and unforgiveness

We become the older brother whenever we respond to life's pains apart from the love of God. Instead of giving forgiveness and mercy to others, we build walls of protection around ourselves. We cling to our bitterness and unforgiveness as if they are some form of defense, but they are not. They are actually prison walls, keeping us from the life of freedom and love God intends.

Unstuck?

Sometimes we get stuck; we do not realize we need to repent. We become blind to our sins and the significance of them. Like the prodigal, who is hungry but not yet desperate for his father's house, we have not come to our senses. Repentance begins with remembering how much God loves us. In one sense it is a gift. In another sense it is a choice.

As we saw in chapter 2, God uses the circumstances of life—relationships we cannot fix, questions we cannot answer and problems we cannot solve—to expose the conditions of our hearts. As we learn to trust Him and respond to His grace in difficult situations, we are able to face what is hidden in our hearts. If we harbor "older brother" sins, we cannot admit how poor and needy and desperate we truly are.

Eventually we may move to a place where we actually want God to expose our hearts. We can then pray with the psalmist: "Search me, O God, and know my heart; test me and know my anxious thoughts. See if there is any offensive way in me, and lead me in the way everlasting" (Psalm 139:23–24). What is that way everlasting? It involves being transformed into more like the father than either of the two sons, learning to love our wayward brothers and sisters with the same mercy God has for us.

Confession and Repentance

One important aspect of repentance is confession. We can be assured that as we sincerely and humbly confess our sins to God, He forgives us and restores us. The Scriptures tell us "if we confess our sins, he is faithful and just and will forgive us our sins and purify us from all unrighteousness" (1 John 1:9).

Honesty in naming and confessing our sins opens a door for God's grace to enter an area of our lives that we had previously closed. His grace is vital to the complete change of direction that repentance calls for. Honest confession breaks our pattern of blindness and dispels the darkness in which evil spirits dwell.

There is power in naming our sins out loud. This will become clearer in the chapter on renunciation, which is a specific expression of repentance.

Repentance and Deliverance

Repentance leads to deeper deliverance from the influence of evil, but it also flows from it. By deliverance I mean the breaking of the power behind habitual patterns of thinking and acting that limit our freedom to accept God's love and turn away from that which blocks His love. Through deliverance we uncover the lies within and expose them for what they are so we may take full responsibility for our lives.

It is so liberating to be able to see hidden sin and deal with it directly. One woman who had ongoing problems with her mother declared with great relief, "Now I know what to call my sin!" A man stood up after a week's seminar to give his testimony. His deliverance came by discovering his sin. "All my life I thought the only sins I could commit were in the Ten Commandments. Now I can confess the sins of my heart." Freedom comes in knowing the names of our enemies, the sins of the heart. It is critical to recognize our sin and to repent. In fact, *there is no freedom apart from repentance.*

A New Reality

"After John was put in prison, Jesus went into Galilee, proclaiming the good news of God. 'The time has come,' he said. 'The kingdom of God is near. Repent and believe the good news!'" (Mark 1:14–15). The first words of Jesus in Mark's gospel are repent, believe and receive. Deeper conversion always involves these three. Nicky Gumble, an Anglican clergyman responsible for the spread of the Alpha course that is reaching millions with the Gospel, reduced the Gospel to the simplest of terms: (1) sorry, (2) thank you and (3) please. All repentance involves the expression of sorrow, the acknowledgment of personal sin and the participation in sin, and asking for forgiveness. Second, conversion requires a "thank you" for what Jesus did in His death and resurrection. And, finally, there is the request (please!) that the Lord come into our lives and reign over our hearts. By living in right relationship to Him, we enter into a new way of living, the new reality, and the kingdom of God.

If you are "stuck," in some way struggling with this whole idea of being a sinner, or you are afraid of the condition of your heart, know that the power that was present when you first turned to the Savior is still present. I suggest, again, that you look not at yourself but at Jesus, the crucified One, who gave Himself for you. Then acknowledge that you are a sinner; be honest and name your sins. Name the sins of the prodigal or the sins of the older brother. If you need help ask the Holy Spirit to guide you as you pray, "Search me, O God, and know my heart! Test me and know my thoughts!" (Psalm 139:23). Pause for a moment and pray:

God exalted him to his own right hand as Prince and Savior
that he might give repentance and forgiveness of sins to Israel.
Acts 5:31

*Lord, I am a sinner; I come before You to tell You I am sorry for
all my sins. Thank You for giving Your life for me, that I might
be forgiven and come home to You. Please come and be Lord of
my life; I want to live in Your kingdom with the freedom of a
child of God. Speak to me as I continue to read this book. Lead
me to the deeper freedom that is found in knowing Your love.*

If we can see the truth about ourselves and not be terrorized
by it, God's reign appears in the simplicity with which we
approach our sins, refusing either to ignore them or make
excuses for them.

Peter John Cameron

In the next chapter I want to share with you how to remove the greatest obstacle to receiving God's forgiveness
and mercy.

4

I Forgive in the Name of Jesus

True reconciliation exposes the awfulness, the abuse, the
pain, the degradation, the truth. . . . It is worthwhile, because
in the end dealing with the real situation helps to bring real
healing.

Bishop Desmond Tutu[1]

Times of Distress

"Would you pray for me? My children can't forgive me," a
woman told me.

"Why not?" I asked.

"Because I never knew how to love them!"

It was a busy conference, with a nonstop schedule of teaching, but we made time to pray for this woman in her pain. After
the next talk on forgiveness, she came to us desperate and angry.
"I cannot forgive my parents for what they did to me."

The next day Lydia told her story. "Seven years ago, when
I turned fifty, I met the Lord. It was the first time I could re-
call experiencing love," she said. As time went on she knew

70

she was not free and could no longer rejoice. The lives of her children confronted her with the reality of her failures. She carried a great burden of guilt. Now that she knew the Lord, she went to ask them to forgive her. Their response: "We cannot forgive you. You never hugged us; you didn't care about us." This was the agony with which she began the conference; it only got worse.

When I spoke about forgiveness, Lydia seethed with rage as she realized her children were right. She failed to communicate her love to them—and she blamed her parents for that. "For fifty years I lived an evil life," she said. "I was the youngest of eight children, and nobody took the time to teach me right from wrong. I was drawn to evil; I did so many evil things. I robbed people, and I had so many abortions I don't remember how many of my children I killed. I divorced my husband and lived with another man.

"Now I understand that it was because my parents never loved me," she continued. "When I consider the way I lived for fifty years and the evil I have done, I am so angry. I cannot forgive."

Reasons We Don't Forgive

Many of us have difficulty forgiving. Almost everyone can call to mind someone he or she needs to forgive deeply. Thinking forgiveness is impossible, we may say "I tried" and then give up. Perhaps we, like Lydia, have gotten in touch with pain and an "I won't" or "I can't" rises up in our hearts. Before we look at the blessing and power of forgiveness, let's summarize some of the reasons we do not allow God's forgiveness to flow through us.

Lack of faith

Because of the depth of our pain we might consider it impossible to forgive. The truth is it is impossible for us, but

God has provided a way. Jesus, speaking about salvation, said to His disciples: "With man this is impossible, but not with God; all things are possible with God" (Mark 10:27).

Lack of "want"

We do not want to forgive because of hurt. We are unwilling to walk through the pain and get to the other side of it, letting it go in forgiveness. This was the case with Lydia. Yet in the depth of her soul she wanted to let go of her anger and forgive. She needed to be understood and accepted before she could forgive.

Lack of awareness of deep wounds

Sometimes we are not aware that there is someone we need to forgive. I had taken someone through forgiveness and deliverance prayer and then asked if anything else came to her mind. "Yes," she replied. "My mom told me that when I was little my older sister was mean to me, hitting me and attacking me on several occasions. Our relationship is fine now, and I do not remember this, but it comes to my mind." Upon pronouncing forgiveness she looked up and declared it was gone. "What is gone?" I asked. She was not sure, but she knew she had been bound and was now set free.

A desire for revenge

We live in a society that wants revenge, not justice. We think we have a right to retaliation. It is generally accepted that the victims of crime want the death penalty for the accused or something worse. Many believers do not know the power of forgiveness, which I will address in a Gospel story later in this chapter.

When Simon was little, his father forced him to be in the room when he was sexually intimate with Simon's mother. Later his dad left. Simon was angry, hurt and confused. Now just beginning to live as a Christian, he found it hard to be pure. He came for help and heard about the importance of forgiveness. No one had ever challenged him to consider his need to forgive. He prayed a prayer of forgiveness and went home to discover that for the first time in years he could look at family pictures with joy and appreciation. I am not aware that he gained victory over sexual temptation that day, but his inner rage was gone.

Fear

We often feel that if we forgive we give up our only defensive weapon. And sometimes we are afraid to give up that weapon. If a young person's only way to deal with sexual abuse is to withdraw into anger, hatred and unforgiveness to maintain a sense of self, the thought of forgiving can involve the fear of losing identity and the means of coping with uncontrollable emotions. If a person is in a threatening situation, forgiveness might be interpreted as not defending oneself and permitting the abuse to continue. This is not the case. Forgiveness does not mean staying in dangerous and abusive situations; it means releasing the blockage to receiving the love of God and being an instrument of His grace. You cannot change the other person, but you can allow the Lord to transform you.

True forgiveness does mean becoming vulnerable again, but it does not mean submersing our human dignity to the abuse of another.

Pride

Sometimes pride, expressed as self-righteousness or self-justification, blocks our forgiveness. Deep down we think we have earned favor with God and, therefore, others need to do something to deserve our forgiveness. When self-justification is at work in us, we become defensive and make excuses. If anyone attacks or accuses us, we have the answer that justifies our action or attitude—all we have put up with and what was done to damage our lives. This strong-looking tower of pride that we hide in is really a hollow defense, and inside we are empty, lonely and fearful.

Failure to take responsibility

We may feel powerless to "fix" a situation: "I am carrying this hurt, and the person who harmed me has the key to unlock it—if he would just repent." Again, we mentally rehearse a scenario of confrontation or reconciliation. Our focus is not really on forgiveness but on resentment and revenge or justification. If someone has hurt us, we need to take full responsibility for our response to whatever has been done to us. It may be right to confront the person for the wrong they did. It is always right to seek reconciliation, but reconciliation begins in *our* hearts. We need to forgive until it is complete. We should start as soon as we recognize the need to forgive, as well as during and after reconciliation, all the time giving thanks to God for the gift of forgiveness (see Psalm 142:1–4).

Influence of evil spirits

In an ideal world our parents would protect us from harm. If we were hurt, their love and faith would enable us to process the pain so we could feel safe again. Later, learning the secrets of God's Kingdom, we would be equipped to face the crosses in our lives, knowing that they are a door to greater trust in God's love. Apart from this grace, we protect ourselves any way we can, by holding on to our anger, vengeance, resentment and bitterness.

Unforgiveness may be our chosen companion, our protector and guard. The same is true for resentment, bitterness, hatred and hurt. When these things are deeply rooted, forgiveness may not be released until we renounce the works of the devil and take authority in the name of Jesus. This was the case for Anna, whom you met in chapter 1. The spirit of unforgiveness needed to be renounced before she could speak the words of forgiveness and receive her freedom.

At other times spirits that enter through past involvement in the occult can act as a seal, keeping other spirits in place and holding us in bondage to unforgiveness (more on this in later chapters).

Lack of understanding of our forgiveness

One more reason we don't forgive is illustrated in the biblical parable of the unmerciful servant, who did not extend the mercy he had been given. Many who were raised in church, taught the truth and live a moral life have never submitted to the Savior, never faced the depth of their sin and never truly received His love. Let's look at this parable closely to better understand how God's mercy toward us relates to our forgiveness of others.

The Relationship Between Forgiveness and Blessing

One day Peter asked Jesus, "'Lord, how many times shall I forgive my brother when he sins against me? Up to seven times?'" Jesus answered, "'I tell you, not seven times, but seventy-seven times'" (Matthew 18:21–22).

In the Scriptures seven is considered the number of completion. Creation was finished and God rested on the seventh day. When Jesus tells us to forgive, He tells us to forgive until it is complete and we find rest. Seventy-seven represents an unlimited number. This is our daily call and often our daily struggle in our commitment to follow Jesus. As painful as it may seem, uncovering hidden unforgiveness, bitterness and resentment in our heart is also the door to freedom.

Jesus continues by telling a parable that the kingdom of heaven is like a king who settles accounts with his servants. He first dealt with a man who owed him "ten thousand talents," which was an unpayable debt, equivalent to millions of dollars. When the servant said he was unable to pay, the master declared that the servant and his family would be sold off as slaves to repay the debt. The servant begged the king, "Please, be patient and merciful, and I will pay you back." The master did take pity, not just providing freedom but also canceling the debt.

But the servant found one of his fellow servants who owed him "a hundred denarii" and he demanded that the debt be paid. This man also begged for patience and mercy, which the servant refused to give. The Gospel says he had the man thrown into prison until he could pay the debt.

News traveled fast, and the master heard about his servant's response. Calling the servant "wicked," he said, "I canceled all that debt of yours because you begged me to. Shouldn't you have had mercy on your fellow servant just as I had on you?" Jesus ends the parable saying, "In anger his master turned him over to the jailers to be tortured, until he should pay back all he owed. This is how my heavenly Father will treat each of you unless you forgive your brother from your heart."

The master ultimately treated the unmerciful servant harshly. Even more shocking is that Jesus tells us our heavenly Father will treat us the same if we do not forgive. Who is the jailer? Satan! What will he do to us? Torment us! Who turns us over to him? God! For what purpose? Read on.

Note closely that the original debt was canceled on the basis of mercy; the servant didn't earn it, he didn't deserve it and it was not because he promised to pay it back. Similarly, we did not earn the forgiveness of sins, nor did we deserve it or receive it based on the promise to pay God back or to be good.

Unfortunately, this man did not *receive* (internalize) the mercy that was given him; he received only what he asked for: the chance to pay it back! Was it a misunderstanding? Or was it his pride, not wishing to give up his right to justify himself? He thought his forgiveness was based on his promise.

I see another parallel here—that we sometimes make unnecessary promises to God and then think our promise is the basis for our forgiveness. But God asks that we give up our right to prove we are worthy of the love He gives to us. Look into your heart. Do you cling to the thought that God loves you because of something you did to deserve it? In our pride and self-delusion we often believe that God loves us and forgives us because of something we did, that we somehow deserve the mercy of God. This deception leaves us in a very vulnerable place. We have been set up for a fall. The results? Every time we fail, we face the whisper of the accuser: "Does God love me?" Instead of superiority, we swing to inferiority and worthlessness. Our response then? Excuses, blame, rationalization and justification for our bad behavior.

The time in prison, being tormented by the devil, has one purpose: to bring us to the point of surrender, where we realize that we can never pay our debt. We need a redeemer to pay the price for our life.

> You foolish Galatians! Who has bewitched you? Before your very eyes Jesus Christ was clearly portrayed as crucified. I would like to learn just one thing from you: Did you receive the Spirit by observing the law, or by believing what you heard? Are you so foolish? After beginning with the Spirit, are you now trying to attain your goal by human effort?
>
> Galatians 3:1–3

Can you relate to this dilemma? I experience it daily. I may begin my day in the Spirit, delighting in His love, submitting to His Word and drawing close in prayer. Then the battle begins. Do I remain in the Spirit, trusting in His goodness and mercy, knowing my debt has been paid? Or do I rely on human effort, justifying my worth based on my ability to pay it back? Do I walk as a son in my Father's house or as a slave simply doing what I must to survive?

The man in this parable did not recognize his need for mercy. He did not ask for it, and when it was given he did not receive it. He only received what he asked for: time to pay it back. He was still a slave to his debt. The call to deeper conversion to Jesus Christ means exposing our desperate need for a Savior who has already paid our un-payable debt; it means making a personal decision to receive the gift and live daily beholding Jesus Christ, crucified for our sins.

We cannot give what we have not received. This servant did not receive mercy and therefore had no mercy to give. It's also true that we cannot receive what we refuse to give! Jesus teaches us that as we ask God to forgive us, *we must be willing to forgive*. And with every blessing God brings into our lives comes the responsibility to use it.

Could Jesus have given a more serious warning than this?

The Power of the Cross

To receive the fullness of the Father's forgiveness, we need to allow the forgiveness of God to flow through us. Jesus was the sacrificial Lamb offered to the Father for our sins. Jesus' crucifixion demonstrates the severity of the wound upon the heart of God, inflicted by Adam and Eve in their sin and perpetuated by our sin. Justice demanded death, but mercy promised a Savior, wounded for our transgressions because of love. Christ crucified is the picture of the justice and mercy of God. There can be no mercy apart from truth. If God were to take away our sin and its consequences, apart from revealing His sacrificial love, we would never know the very nature of God, which is love.

Only through the cross can we grasp the greatness of God's love; the power of the cross is the power of forgiveness. When we truly experience the power of the Gospel, which is forgiveness, our lives are changed.

I pray that out of his glorious riches he may strengthen you with power through his Spirit in your inner being, so that Christ may dwell in your hearts through faith. And I pray that you, being rooted and established in love, may have power, together with all the saints, to grasp how wide and long and high and deep is the love of Christ, and to know this love that surpasses knowledge—that you may be filled to the measure of all the fullness of God.

Ephesians 3:16–19

In the parable we just examined, the unmerciful servant is sent to prison "until he should pay back all he owed." How unreasonable this seems. It's a debt that can never be paid. His only way out is to change the basis by which he relates to the king, to plead for mercy and no longer rely upon his ability or desire to pay it back. This is our situation. We need to face the rebellion that says, "I want to do it myself" and replace it with, "Thank You for the gift; I surrender to Your love."

This is where forgiveness is born; this is the source, the love of Christ. What is released? The gift of love. As we receive forgiveness, we are empowered to forgive.

The Gift of Love

The apostle Paul had great love and great zeal. He understood the mysteries of the Kingdom as well as anyone who ever lived. In 1 Timothy 1:15 he said, "Here is a trustworthy saying that deserves full acceptance: Christ Jesus came into the world to save sinners—of whom I am the worst."

In Luke 7 Jesus was visiting a Pharisee named Simon.

When a woman who had lived a sinful life in that town learned that Jesus was eating at the Phariseee's house, she brought an alabaster jar of perfume, and as she stood behind him at his feet weeping, she began to wet his feet with her tears.

Then she wiped them with her hair, kissed them and poured perfume on them.

Luke 7:38–39

Knowing the contempt his host held for this woman and how she had suffered the reproach of men like him for years, Jesus spoke—and His words brought conviction to the Pharisees and healing to the heart of the woman. He told another parable about payment of debts. One man owed a moneylender five hundred denarii. Another man owed fifty. Neither could pay, and the moneylender canceled both debts. Which of them will love the moneylender more? Simon replied, "I suppose the one who had the bigger debt canceled" (Luke 7:43). Right, said Jesus.

The person who loves God more is the one who understands the depth of his sin and the meaning of God's sacrifice. A superficial understanding of these mysteries leaves one with a superficial love.

Jesus had more to say to Simon the Pharisee. He pointed out the woman's loving acts, saying,

> "You did not give me any water for my feet, but she wet my feet with her tears and wiped them with her hair. You did not give me a kiss, but this woman, from the time I entered, has not stopped kissing my feet. You did not put oil on my head, but she has poured perfume on my feet. Therefore, I tell you, her many sins have been forgiven—for she loved much. But he who has been forgiven little loves little." Then Jesus said to [the woman], "Your sins are forgiven."

Luke 7:44–48

How did Jesus know her sins were forgiven? As the Son of God, He may have known it by revelation, or He may have known it by the natural observation of her behavior. She was not bound by bitterness, anger and unforgiveness, even though she was in the company of those who had made her life miserable. What is the sign that sins have been forgiven? An outpouring of love, generosity, affection and humility. The one who knows the depth of our debt to God and has received His mercy is the one who has great love. Jesus could see—and invites us to see—that those who love find the source of that love in God.

Do you wish to love more? Forgive more deeply! All healing flows from forgiveness. The love of God is demonstrated to the extreme in Jesus, the sinless One, taking our sins upon Himself and giving His life for us. The one who loves deeply is the one who knows the significance of that love and becomes a vessel of forgiveness to others. What is love if it is not the love of God poured into our hearts by the Holy Spirit (see Romans 5:5)? Love is the gift of God.

Love is also a command. Jesus gives us some very practical advice about how to love those who hurt us. "But I tell you who hear me: Love your enemies, do good to those who hate you, bless those who curse you, pray for those who mistreat you" (Luke 6:27–28).

As I noted in chapter 1, to bless means to speak well about someone, wanting that person to prosper. To pray for someone is to touch God's love for that person, asking God to bless him. If you find forgiveness is not complete, don't give up. Humble yourself before the Lord and do what He has commanded until it is done. One clear sign that forgiveness has taken place is a new appreciation for the person and gratitude toward God for the gift this person has been in your life.

The Secret of Forgiveness

At another conference, when the guest speaker placed his hands on a middle-aged woman and prayed for her, she fell to the ground, thrashing around, manifesting what may have been a bondage to evil spirits. The pastor asked for my assistance, explaining that she was a very respected woman in her church. We took the woman out of the limelight, to a private place, and with a little encouragement she came out of the agitated state. I asked her what was happening.

"I don't know," she said.

"What is going on in your life right now? What is causing you turmoil?" I asked.

"My son is causing me trouble." Her description of his disrespectful behavior made it obvious this was a source of great pain for her.

"Tell me about your husband," I encouraged.

"My husband left. One day he said he was going to the store, and he never came home."

"What about your father?" I continued.

"He was violent and abusive. My parents divorced."

"Do you want to be free?" I asked. She said yes, definitely.

"Are you willing to forgive?" I probed. I led her through a prayer forgiving her son, her husband and then her dad for his violence and abuse. There seemed to be something more. "Is there anything else you would like to forgive?" I asked. With deep emotion, she breathed out the words, "I forgive my dad for leaving me." The weight lifted. The power was broken. She renounced abandonment, rejection and fear of abandonment, and then commanded those spirits to go. She was free.

Satan's plan was exposed. The depth of rejection and pain from her father's leaving had locked her in a prison, keeping her bound by her hurt and unforgiveness. Over time the same pattern—and the deep fear that another man would abandon her—reproduced itself, first in her husband and then in the trouble with her son. It is not unusual to find the deepest hurt buried beneath other memories. She needed to deal with her husband's leaving and her father's violence before she faced the deepest trauma: her father's abandonment of her as a young girl. We prayed for the Spirit's filling and healing, and she left with new hope and trust in God as her Father.

Wounded, suffering, rejected, the crucified Jesus prayed, "Father, forgive them, for they do not know what they are doing" (Luke 23:34). God, by the Word made flesh, eternally speaks these words. They are active and alive, never far from us. Do you want to forgive? The secret of forgiveness is found in Jesus Christ crucified. It is His Word, it is His power; you belong to Him and His Spirit is in you.

To forgive you need two things. The first is willingness. The second is faith. How much faith? Faith the size of a very tiny mustard seed can move mountains, Jesus says. "Nothing will be impossible for you" (Matthew 17:20). Forgiveness may seem like that mountain; it may seem impossible. You may feel like you don't want to go there again because of the pain. Please don't stop. Jesus came to set the prisoners free.

Some people tell me, "I can say the words, but I feel like a hypocrite because forgiveness is not in my heart." In some cases forgiveness does seem humanly impossible. All we can do is make an act of the will, speak the words (which breaks the power of the enemy) and trust that the Lord will do the rest.

Refusing to forgive is a sin for which we need to repent and ask God's forgiveness. The words of Jesus are so powerful and urgent: "But if you *do not forgive* men their sins, your Father will not *forgive* your sins" (Matthew 6:15, emphasis added). Rarely have I heard the sin of unforgiveness listed with great and awful sins. Yet the words of Jesus about unforgiveness are so strong that many would rather avoid them, denying their power and escaping from the responsibility of forgiving.

Six Steps to Unlocking Forgiveness

As I wind up this chapter, allow me to give six clear steps for unlocking the door of forgiveness.

1. Find someone you trust to pray with you. It helps if this person is spiritually mature. Look for someone who has suffered as a Christian and been made stronger for it; someone you know has had to forgive; someone with whom you feel safe. This same person may assist you in responding to the message of the next three chapters.

2. Begin to praise God and thank Him. "Enter his gates with thanksgiving and his courts with praise" (Psalm 100:4). Ask the Holy Spirit to lead you.

3. When you sense His presence, consider Jesus, the author and perfecter of our faith. Acknowledge His love and His power.

   As a believer you have identified with Him, you have given Him your life and your life has been hidden in Him. The Holy Spirit lives in you. Areas where you have not forgiven are areas you have not surrendered to the One who loves you. Pray out loud, "Lord Jesus, please forgive me for trying to save my life, for not trusting you." Humble yourself.

4. Remember the words of Jesus: "Father forgive them— they know not what they are doing." These are eternal words, and He has given them to you. The Eternal One is willing to release the power of those words again through you.

5. Think of the person who hurt you and what that person did. Let yourself feel the pain. Forgiveness takes a deeper hold on us as we forgive from the place of pain. To say you forgive while denying the pain does not deal with the root. Once you have gotten in touch with the pain, say out loud: "In the name of Jesus, I forgive _____ for _____." Say the name of the person or describe the person (the man with the dark jacket who attacked me outside of my home two years ago). Then be very specific in what you are forgiving the person for. There are at least two reasons to say it out loud. First, it helps you focus and keeps you from

being vague. Second, you can listen to yourself. You can tell if you are being real or not. If you trust the person praying with you, you may ask him or her to help you be specific. If that person has discernment or empathy, he or she may be able to give you words that help you. For example, "I forgive _____ for humiliating me and rejecting me and making me feel worthless."

Have your friend pray that the love of God would release you and make you a vessel of His love. Repeat these steps if others come to your mind whom you need to forgive.

If you have difficulty speaking declarations of forgiveness, try speaking to the Lord about your hurt and pain. Let Him lead you to the place of forgiveness. He will. I suggested this to Lydia, who did not believe she could forgive her parents or even say the words. I asked her to tell Jesus how angry and hurt she was. She later told me she tried to say, "I don't want to forgive them," but instead the words "I forgive my parents" came out. As she prayed, God worked through her. Upon saying the words she began to weep and express sorrow that her parents were never loved and did not know any better. "I realized how miserable they were," she said, glimpsing their own pain for the first time.[2]

Ask God to bring others to your mind. One or two is plenty to start with, since you need to be willing to touch the pain. (You may find that you need to take the next step of renunciation, which is found in the next chapter.) Remember, we should not ask for more than we are willing to give. With every blessing God brings into our life comes the responsibility to use it in accordance with His plan for us.

6. Give thanks to God for His goodness, and ask Him to direct your paths. Use your newfound freedom to love someone in a practical way. The fruit of forgiveness is love.[3]

Don't Forget Yourself!

I cannot say this better than my friend:

Neal,

*It was great to see you the other day. I don't know
if you noticed, but I couldn't help but smile while
we prayed as I declared victory in the name of Jesus
over the sins and struggles in my life. Christ had some
monumental victories in my heart the other day. Thank
you for answering my questions and thank you for
praying with me. I actually learned just as much when
we prayed as when we talked. Also, the other day I
was in my kitchen about to go upstairs to spend time
with God, and I remembered your asking me if I felt
guilty. After thinking about it, I realized I had forgiven
everyone and repented of my sins, but I still hadn't
forgiven myself. Anyway, I spent some time yesterday
forgiving myself out loud. It was awesome. Thanks
again, I'll talk to you soon. You are in my prayers.*

With love from your brother in Christ,

Mike

To forgive yourself is simply a declaration that you are in agreement with God, that you will not hold yourself to higher standards than God, and you will not demand of yourself more than He does. We forgive ourselves the same way God does, on the basis of the mercy poured out in Jesus.

We know we have forgiven when we begin to realize that the person who has offended us is really a source of blessing. God gives us the gift of gratitude. In the same way, forgiving ourselves allows us to appreciate who we are and how God made us.

Jesus said, "This is my blood of the covenant, which is poured out for many for the forgiveness of sins" (Matthew 26:28). *Do you believe this?*

> Then he took the cup, gave thanks and offered it to them, saying, "Drink from it, all of you. This is my blood of the covenant, which is poured out for many for the forgiveness of sins."
>
> Matthew 26:27–28

Jesus, You died for me that I could be forgiven and the door to reconciliation with the Father would be opened. You revealed Your love for me while I was still in sin. You gave Your life as a holy sacrifice for me. Give me the courage to forgive and the faith to trust that what You have given me I can give to others.

> But God demonstrates his own love for us in this: While we were still sinners, Christ died for us.
>
> Romans 5:8

In the next chapter you will discover how to add power to your repentance.

5

I Renounce in the Name of Jesus

Therefore, O king, be pleased to accept my advice: Renounce
your sins by doing what is right, and your wickedness by being
kind to the oppressed. It may be that then your prosperity
will continue.

Daniel 4:27

Jamie's Story

"When I tell people about God, I tell them that He loves
them and that He will change their lives. Usually we see Him
change our lives over time, but because of the power of the
prayer you and I had together, I also tell them that sometimes
He just does it!"

This is what Jamie told me three years after we prayed for
her. We met Jamie when she was sixteen. She was causing
a lot of trouble in her youth group, constantly doing things
to make people reject her. She intimidated others. Using
emotions, she manipulated and controlled everyone around
her. Friends told her she had to stop acting like this, but she

couldn't. It came to a head after she and another girl (who was not committed to Christ) went outside the youth group meeting and yelled profanity at them through the window. Her life was a contradiction. This brought it to a crisis.

"The day I came for prayer I drove around the block what seems like a hundred times," she said. "I was really scared at the thought of talking to somebody about myself. But I had a big fight with my youth group leader. He confronted me and made it clear I had to change. I had given my life to Christ a year and a half before, but until the day we prayed, it didn't go anywhere."

When we met Jamie, she seemed a bit nervous and distracted. She kept fixing her hair and shifting her position. In the middle of our conversation, she took out and applied her Chapstick. I wondered if we could help her. She was a young evangelical Christian with no idea about evil spirits. If I had told her about deliverance prayer, she might not have come. My goal was to love her and help her feel safe. I'd only go through doors that she opened.

Jamie told me she approached life with an "I don't care" attitude. She told me that her mom had a drinking problem and was separated from Jamie's birth father. In addition, Jamie did things to make others dislike her, even though she didn't really want to; this contradiction was a form of self-sabotage.

After listening for a while, I restated what I had heard and tried to communicate that I understood. I pointed out how she was protecting herself by rejecting people before they could reject her. "It seems like you have a big fear of being vulnerable. You give everyone a reason to reject you because you're afraid of being hurt," I explained carefully.

Three years later she explained it this way: "When you described the way I was living, it was the first time I ever saw what was going on in me objectively. Every day of my life I had just lived this pattern and never thought about it.

My perception of God and the Gospel were twisted by my patterns of thinking.

"My mind was always running, always thinking, controlling, manipulating and keeping God from coming too close to my heart. I kept God away from my feelings about others. I would not admit to God or myself when I got hurt. I would not talk to Him about my hurt. Even with God, I acted as though I didn't care.

"I didn't trust. I didn't let people know me because I was afraid. Deep down, I was just waiting for God to reject me or tell me He didn't like me. So I pushed away everyone who reached out to me. I would make people mad at me on purpose. I didn't want to give anyone a chance to hurt me. So I didn't let anyone get to know me. That way, if they rejected me and never really knew me, I could just say I don't care. If I let myself care, it would hurt more. I had a problem thinking that if God got to my heart, He would use it against me or that He would not like me."

When Jamie came for prayer, I did not mention spirits at all. I just asked her to say, "In the name of Jesus, I renounce control, manipulation, fear. . . ." They were easy for her to say. "Now renounce rejection," I instructed her. She hesitated and looked as though she saw something for the first time. "That is big, isn't it?" I said. She admitted that it was.

Later she explained, "As soon as I said, 'I renounce rejection in the name of Jesus' I felt a change. It was like I surrendered to God for the first time. I had been trying to give my problems to Christ. I agreed with others when they said, 'You have to stop acting like this,' but I did not know how. After renouncing rejection, I felt such relief. It was one of the first times I ever quieted myself in Christ. I never knew His peace before that moment."

After Jamie renounced everything we had listed, I commanded everything she had renounced to leave in the name of Jesus. Then we prayed for blessing on her life. I left her follow-up in the hands of her youth leader.

We heard about the change. We heard that every time she gave her testimony, she told the story about how Christ came to her that day we prayed.

She continued, "I still struggle with some of the same problems, but now I deal with them and I know that I am growing. I have some of the same habits, but now I build relationships and communicate. I am not paralyzed with fear, thinking that people will not accept me."

In Jamie's story I see a three-part process: (a) Confronting her about her life. There was a crisis. She could no longer stay where she was; (b) Exposing to the light her patterns of thinking and behaving; (c) Renouncing the enemy and exposing its identity. As Jamie spoke she could see for the first time the spirit of rejection. It was not she. She did not have to live that way; she could be separated from the influence of the spirit of rejection.

One of the problems with deliverance ministry has been incorporating it into the broader Christian life. Many believe it to be a one-time event, isolated from normal Christian growth. But, in reality, for Jamie it started when she met the Lord in a personal way and perhaps long before that as God reached out to her. Jamie is still growing, so the end of her story has yet to be written. She is in God's hands.

Renunciation

"I renounce Satan and all of his works and all of his empty promises. . . ." These words date back to the fourth-century Church as part of the liturgical formula used at baptism. Many churches continue to use these words at baptisms and baptismal renewals today. In the fourth century, the baptismal ceremony was an expression of all that happened in the life of the candidate as he or she came to Christ. It was a symbolic expression of how the candidate was being transferred from the kingdom of darkness to the Kingdom of the beloved Son (see Colossians 1:13). These words followed three years of preparation in which prayers for exorcism were regularly prayed. At baptism, on the eve of Easter, the candidates stood and faced the west, a symbol for the kingdom of darkness because it is where the sun sets, releasing darkness on the earth. Then they publicly renounced Satan. It was an expression of many renunciations that had already transpired.

Renouncing means declaring that you want no more to do with this influence in your life; it is over. You want no more lies, no more empty promises. Renunciation is an expression of repentance that many believers rarely use. Renunciation does three things:

1. *Identifies the lie and the power behind the lie.* Jamie's life shifted toward freedom as the root issue was exposed. As we explained to Jamie the effect her father's leaving early in life may have had on her and her pattern of self-protection by destructive behavior, we exposed the roots of her problems. Jamie began to see herself as separate from the way she was living. Her power over this destructive lifestyle came when she identified the root of rejection, named it and renounced it. Then she could feel its power and recognize it as something that was not she.[1]

2. *Breaks the power.* Many of us who believe in God's love revealed in Christ fail to recognize that areas of our hearts are still bound. This is the truth: If we belong to Jesus Christ, we live by grace and are free. Yet evil spirits still influence us and seek to make a home in areas of our lives that we have not fully surrendered to the truth. They need a legal right to hold areas of our lives in bondage. That legal right is based on the fact that in some way they have been "invited in." Renunciation is how we give notice that they must vacate, that their lease has been terminated. It is how we open the door and show them the way out. Sometimes, as in the case

of Jamie, showing them the door is all that's needed. Most often you need not only to open the door and cancel the lease, but also to command them to leave. (We'll address this further in chapter 6.) But once their identity is exposed and the entryway has been sealed (repentance, forgiveness, renunciation), they must go.

3. *Gives us personal responsibility.* Renouncing our enemies is an expression of our human dignity and freedom. It is an act of cooperating with the saving work of Jesus. It expresses that we have taken responsibility for our life. We stand as adults looking at the enemy and telling him, "It is over. I have had enough. I know where you are hiding, and you cannot hide there anymore."

Guilt, Responsibility and Fear

The confusion between responsibility and guilt can create an obstacle to getting free. We do not have to judge our culpability, even when we take responsibility for wrongdoing. Even if we are to blame, God is not looking to place blame on us. He simply wants to free us. The issue is our willingness to take responsibility for our own life. Do I wish to remain a victim or take hold of my human dignity and walk in freedom? (I don't mean to minimize the process—it is never simple—but I do want to underscore the principle.)

The responsibility is ours. Did you ever stand up to someone who bullied you as a kid? I did. When I was six years old, I was intimidated and frustrated by a local bully. One day I was able to get past his reach and get a punch in. He was shocked; I felt super. I remember how good I felt as I raided my piggy bank and walked down to the local candy store to buy a soda. There is great freedom in finally standing up to a bully. Strength comes and fear is drained as we expose the lie and take up who we are. Things changed after that day: The attack, the intimidation, was never the same again.

Many of us have been bullied by lies and fears all our lives. Great relief comes when we finally realize we do not have to be afraid and we have the power to do something about our situations.

In the case of abuse, the victim is lost in a maze of shame, blame, anger and rage; the person may be surrounded by a sense of helplessness. As believers we are no longer helpless; we have the power of the Kingdom in our lives. We renounce not simply by our own authority, but in the name of Jesus, the One who has been given all authority in heaven and in earth (see Matthew 28:18).

Often on weeklong conferences, I lead the group in a time of renunciation. I pray about a list of spirits to be renounced, and I invite those who want to participate with me to renounce the spirits they recognize at work in their lives. We go on for about five minutes saying, "I renounce fear in the name of Jesus, I renounce lust . . . I renounce. . . ."

As we do it, a sense of new strength comes to the group. Fear is drained as we exercise the awareness of who we are in Christ. Tangible relief settles over the group, for each one realizes, "I can speak against my enemies without fear!"

Our Words Have Power

Did you ever try to start a diet without telling somebody? If so, you probably never got very far. We reveal our divided hearts when we fail to speak our commitment. If you speak and your heart is divided, you will hear yourself and be convicted of having a divided heart. The words "I am going to lose weight" have tremendous power.

Coach Bill McCartney, founder of the Promise Keepers men's movement, once told a story about how he was taking the Colorado State football team to its biggest game ever. To prepare the team he asked his players to reflect on what they were going to do. Then each player would come before the coach and tell him exactly what he was going to do on game day. The team played better that day than anyone could have expected. The message: "Have a good man tell you what he is going to do, and he will do it." Words have power; they reveal the heart. They expose and confront and defeat double-mindedness.

More than Just Words

The people of the Old Testament had a deep appreciation for the power of the spoken word. God's Word has its source in the depths of God: It reveals His personality, and it is one with God. Yet it is also distinct from God. God's Word has the power to bring about what it means.

Man's words reveal his personality and his heart. The Hebrew people took words very seriously. Once a word was spoken, it had the power to bring about what it meant. A word spoken became a real power, a separate entity. It could not be destroyed or changed. Isaac mistakenly gave his blessing to Jacob. When he found out that he was mistaken, he could not take it back and give it to Esau.

It is a privilege to speak in the name of Jesus. To speak in His name means to speak in His character and in His personality, in union with His Spirit. When we say, "I forgive or renounce in the name of Jesus," these words have power to bring about what they signify. Do not underestimate the power of the spoken word.

Demons cannot read our minds. It is not good enough simply to think, "I renounce this or that." It is when they hear such words that they know their power is broken and they submit. When we speak the truth of God's Word with our voices, we destroy strongholds.

Jesus knew the power of the spoken word. With a word or a simple command, He cast out demons, healed the sick, raised the dead and calmed the sea. He didn't just pray silently or think things into being. Rather, He said, "Be cured"; "Lazarus, come out"; "Be still"; "Get up and walk." And the spoken word brought about the reality it signified.

An interpreter once asked me, "Why don't you just have everyone renounce all these things?" without naming them specifically or without any personal resonance with the issue at hand, as if mere words alone broke the enemy's power. Just as forgiveness of others takes a deeper hold on us when we forgive from the place of pain, we have greater authority when we renounce evil spirits from a place of revelation. Revelation of how a spirit is at work moves one from just saying words to speaking to the heart of the issue with power. When I took the whole group through a time of renunciation, some people received significant help because of what God had already revealed to them. Others expressed a general sense of newness. One man said, "I feel as though I have taken a spiritual shower."

Key Questions

What do you want Jesus to do for you? That is one of the questions I often ask people when they come for prayer. Based on their response, I try to help them understand what Jesus wants them to do. I help them understand the importance of repentance, forgiveness and renunciation.

What does Jesus want you to do?

Why not start naming your enemies—those things in your heart that keep you from the freedom you have in Christ? Things like greed, pride, hatred and bitterness. When you name them you gain authority over them. Name them according to their identities or what they do. You started this in chapter 3 when you identified sins of the heart. When these sins have a deep hold on you and you are compulsive about them, it is a good thing to renounce them as your enemies.

You don't need to decide how deeply rooted they are in your life. You don't need to become introspective and try to heal yourself. But you can list the areas of your weakness, especially areas marked by hopelessness and compulsion. Then you can look at them prayerfully and say, "Lord, show me the roots." What are Satan's plans for my life, and how can I take responsibility for my life and break his power?"

Trust Jesus with your life. He will show you what you need. If you find yourself going down a spiral of unhealthy introspection, stop thinking and start talking out loud to the One who saved you. Find your spiritually mature friend. Remember, "For where two or three come together in my name, there am I with them" (Matthew 18:20). Don't go deeper than you are ready to go. Let Jesus lead you.

> Therefore say to the house of Israel, "This is what the Sovereign LORD says: Repent! Turn from your idols and renounce all your detestable practices!"
>
> *Ezekiel 14:6*

> *Lord Jesus, I surrender my life to You. I trust in You. In the name of Jesus I renounce Satan and all his works and empty promises. In the name of Jesus I renounce selfishness, pride, lust, greed and self-rejection. . . .*
>
> *Thank You, Jesus, for giving me victory over my enemies. I am not afraid.*

How much authority do you need to drive out a spirit? As you will see in the next chapter, if you believe in Jesus and understand the principles, you have all the authority you need.

6

I Take Authority in the Name of Jesus

Hence the Lord has said that he who has faith the size of a mustard seed can move a mountain by a word of command (Matthew 17:20), that is, he can destroy the devil's dominion over us and remove it from its foundation.

Maximos the Confessor

It Has to Go!

"You have renounced a spirit of hatred, we have commanded it to leave and it has to go unless there is some basic issue that has not been dealt with." It was the end of the day, and we had spent two hours interviewing and praying with Monica. Several times she had said she was at peace, and we were about to end the session.

There was, however, no evidence that the release was complete. Our hearts went out to Monica, and we desperately wanted to see the Lord set her free. But we were very tired and realized that only God knows the depths of a person; we have to respect His timetable. As we were saying good-bye

98

she revealed something we knew necessitated more prayer. "I still have fear in my heart."

She had renounced fear and we had commanded it to leave. It had to leave. So why hadn't it? If this had happened years ago, I would have thought, "I have to be more forceful in commanding the devil to leave. If I were holier or more anointed, it would leave. If another person were praying, it would not take so long." All of those things may be true in part. The greater the anointing, and the more authority the person praying has received, the faster the power of the enemy is exposed and broken. But I have learned that the level of spiritual authority a person has is secondary to exposing the lie and having the person renounce the spirit behind the lie.

With this in mind, I asked Monica to sit down once more. I told her very directly that if fear was still present, there must be a reason. I instructed her, "Monica, I want you to close your eyes and get in touch with that fear. Let your mind go back to any time in your life when you felt such fear." Her mind focused on sitting at the family dinner table with her dad. She had already prayed to forgive her dad; there was no fresh insight.

From the beginning of our session I had a mental picture of her in a prison. As she renounced many things I felt as though the prison gate opened. I could imagine that Jesus went in to get her, but she was not ready to leave with Him. We did not want to fall into the trap of trying too hard, which could cause her to become introspective. Once again we brought the session to a close and began a prayer of blessing. As we did, the thought came to me: *control.*

"Could you renounce a spirit of control?" I asked. After she did, I added, "In the name of Jesus I command control and every spirit that she has renounced to leave." In my mind I saw Monica leave the jail and enter a meadow. I asked her what happened. "I see myself in a meadow with Jesus," she said. She received her blessing, and I learned another lesson. I knew from experience that deep fears in a person's life often lead to a problem with control. Even though she did not hint at it in the interview, I should have asked some questions about it. If you pray with others seeking to set them free, you will always find opportunities to confess your weakness.

Understanding Authority

One day the chief priests and elders asked Jesus, "By what authority are you doing these things? And who gave you this authority?" (Matthew 21:23). This question, meant as a trap for Jesus, can be useful for us to ask. A key to freedom from the influence of evil spirits is understanding authority and where it comes from.

Authority is the power to act on behalf of somebody else. It is something that belongs to another. We carry that power because it has been given to us. After His resurrection, Jesus said to His disciples, "All authority in heaven and on earth has been given to me. Therefore go . . ." (Matthew 28:18–20). Jesus had been given authority. How much authority? All authority in heaven and earth. He was one with the Father, and He was the Father's representative. He had it all. He healed the sick, forgave sins and proclaimed the Kingdom of God by the authority He had been given. The authority of Jesus amazed the people. They said to one another, "What is this teaching? With authority and power he gives orders to evil spirits and they come out!" (Luke 4:36). They had never seen anything like it.

Matthew 8:5–10 tells us of a Roman soldier who understood how authority works. He asked Jesus to heal his servant, paralyzed and in pain. Jesus quickly said He'd go find the servant and heal him. But the centurion replied:

> "Lord, I do not deserve to have you come under my roof. But just say the word, and my servant will be healed. For I myself am a man under authority, with soldiers under me. I tell this one, 'Go,' and he goes; and that one, 'Come,' and he comes.

I say to my servant, 'Do this,' and he does it." When Jesus heard this he was astonished and said to those following him, "I tell you the truth, I have not found anyone in Israel with such great faith."

Matthew 8:5–10

The centurion understood the power of a word spoken by someone under authority. He knew the authority Jesus carried came from God and that it was limitless. Therefore, Jesus just had to say the word. Jesus saw his faith, expressed in deep humility, as remarkable.

Jesus had authority as the Son of God. He did not need someone else's name to cast out demons. Even so, Jesus understood authority. He did only what was given to Him to do, and He spoke only what He received from His Father. "For I have not spoken on my own authority; the Father who sent me has himself given me commandment what to say and what to speak" (John 12:49, RSV). He walked in the knowledge that He was sent. He knew that He drove out demons by the power of God. "If I drive out demons by the finger of God, then the kingdom of God has come to you" (Luke 11:20).

In Relationship, Jesus Has Given Us Authority

In the course of His ministry, Jesus gave authority to the Twelve and to a group of 72 to cast out demons; He sent them out to proclaim the Kingdom. The context for casting out demons was to advance the Kingdom of God and to destroy the works of the devil.

The authority anyone carries does not belong to that person. Rather, it belongs to the one who gave it. You and I are God's representatives. It is our relationship with Him that enables us to exercise authority. A policeman carries the authority of the police force. He carries the badge and wears the uniform, which indicates he represents those who entrusted it to him. If he did not have these symbols indicating he was under authority, his words and actions would not carry the same weight.

Only in union with Jesus Christ, and in His name, do we carry authority in the spirit world. In Acts 19:13–15, Luke tells us of seven men who tried to invoke the name of Jesus over demons. They said, "In the name of Jesus, whom Paul preaches, I command you to come out." But an evil spirit answered them, "Jesus I know, and I know about Paul, but who are you?" Demons recognize the name of Jesus and must respond. But they did not recognize the authority of the Lord in these men as they obviously did in the apostle Paul. Perhaps the seven men were moving in an area where they were not invited or authorized by God, or perhaps they did not know Jesus but simply knew that the name of Jesus had power.

Our authority is in our relationship with Christ. Are you confident in His love? Are you in personal relationship with others who are pursuing their relationship with the Lord?[1] If not, go back and reflect on chapter 2.

Later, to His disciples, Jesus said:

> "All authority in heaven and on earth has been given to me. Therefore go and make disciples of all nations, baptizing them in the name of the Father and of the Son and of the Holy Spirit, and teaching them to obey everything I have commanded you. And surely I am with you always, to the very end of the age."
>
> Matthew 28:18–20

He has the authority to send us, and if we are sent we carry His authority. What's more, the One in whom all author-ity on heaven and earth rests goes with us. "I am with you always." The authority of His words and the work of Jesus continue in us, because He sent us forth as His instruments in this world. He wants to bring the Good News to every human being, and He wants each of us to take our place in doing so. In John 20:21 Jesus said, "Peace be with you! As the Father has sent me, I am sending you." Jesus carried the authority of the Father, and now we carry the authority of the Son. We gain more authority as we bring more areas of our lives under His authority. The more you have surrendered, the more you can be an instrument.

You Have Been Given Authority over Evil Spirits

Mark's gospel also ends with Jesus telling the eleven disciples to go into the entire world to preach the Good News. His word to them is also His word to us.

> "And these signs will accompany those who believe: In my name they will drive out demons; they will speak in new tongues; they will pick up snakes with their hands; and when they drink deadly poison, it will not hurt them at all; they will place their hands on sick people, and they will get well."
>
> Mark 16:17–18

We have been given authority in His name to advance the Kingdom of God. We can exercise this authority over evil spirits as we serve Him, first in our own lives. We are responsible for our lives. Often the first person we need to share the good news with is ourselves. What we have accepted as truth needs to go deeper until it transforms our lives. The truth exposes the lies we believe and sets us free from our bondage. Second, those who have children have a great responsibility to raise them in the truth and protect them from the influence of evil spirits. Third, we must bring light to those who have entrusted themselves to us. When someone comes to you for prayer, telling you secrets, you are invited in as a representative of Christ, an instrument of the love and mercy of God. Finally, some have been given responsibility in the Church and in society. God has given them authority to lead in such a way as to expose and destroy the works of the devil. (The principles in part 1 of this book are meant to help you take responsibility for your life and respond to Jesus. Part 2 shows how to apply these principles to help others be set free from the influence of evil spirits.)

Taking Authority

"The time has come," Jesus said. "The Kingdom of God is near. Repent and believe the good news!" (see Mark 1:15). The Good News invitation is not simply to leave behind the world and the kingdom of darkness, but to enter into our inheritance, the Kingdom of the beloved Son. We do that by faith. What good is it to repent from all your sins and renounce the works of the devil, yet remain in the prison that has held you captive? If Jesus has unlocked the prison door, is it not time to push it open and come out to a new life?

The act of taking authority over evil spirits is a necessary part of the deliverance process. Taking authority over the enemy and his works in your life is an expression of your faith, what you believe, what you believe about Jesus and what you believe about your relationship to Him.

We know we are responsible for our lives and our children's lives. When we believe the enemy is at work, we have the authority to command him to leave. *Yet wisdom tells us that the word of command is not isolated from the rest of the Christian life.* Living our life as a disciple of the Lord is the substance of our growing liberty. If we do not deal with the root causes and receive affirmation and blessing for our lives, we can be driving the devil out through a revolving door. He goes because we command him to go in the name of Jesus, but he comes right back. "I know you are telling me to go, but, see, I have this invitation, sent by you," he says confidently.

When we take authority over any spirit that has had its entryway sealed, its invitation canceled, it has to leave. But demons are not going to leave if we say "out" with our mouths and "stay" with our hearts. Standing with Jesus, we have His authority over the devil. But we do not have the right to expect the devil to leave where he has been welcomed. What good is it to tell a spirit of lust to leave if you are unwilling to get rid of the pornography hidden under your bed? I heard about one man who told his pastor that before he'd go into an adult bookstore, he always took authority over the devil so he would not get into bondage. What foolishness!

A Word of Command

After you have responded to the call to believe, repent, forgive and renounce, the next step of taking authority is very simple and powerful. Once you are in the presence of the Lord, preferably with that mature friend, say out loud in a firm voice, "In the name of Jesus I break the power of every evil spirit that I have renounced, and I command them to leave now." If you have some areas of particular weakness, say, "I break the power of (i.e., selfishness, greed . . .), and I command it to leave now." We must say it out loud, because we are not merely performing a human ritual; we are actually speaking to demons. Speaking is an expression of our faith.

The things that oppress us often are precisely the things that keep us from knowing we have authority over them in the name of Jesus. Worthlessness, pride, unbelief—whatever the enemies are, they all work to keep us from understanding and exercising authority over them. Because of this it is usually helpful (especially if it is the first time) and often necessary to have someone else say with us or for us the word of command.

Hearing a command given with the authority of Jesus imparts to us a sense of His authority. It drives away our fears. It exposes unbelief in us and brings an awareness that we really are dealing with demons. Someone with experience can impart a deeper level of faith that the enemy must go in the name of Jesus. No teacher? No one to help? God can handle it. Find a pastor or mature friend and share this book with him or her. Trust God, and He will do the rest.

Never speak a word of command thinking that it is your anointing or your authority. It is Jesus manifesting His power through you. In spiritual conflict we should always be aware that Jesus is advancing the Kingdom of God through us. If we look at ourselves, trying to estimate the authority we have, we will surely fail. We always rebuke evil spirits in the name of Jesus. To speak in the name of Jesus means to act in the person, character and Spirit of Jesus. Whenever I give a command, I always remember that I am simply His instrument.[2]

A word of caution: If you know you have deep levels of spiritual bondage, seek help from your pastor first. Spend time with a mature friend discussing and praying through the previous few chapters. Then you may take authority; but to be safe take authority only over what you have renounced. If evil spirits manifest and there is no relief, do not keep commanding them to go. Tell them to stop hassling you, and set your eyes on Jesus. Take control of yourself and seek out someone with experience. Remember, you are in God's hands. "Look at the birds of the air; they do not sow or reap or store away in barns, and yet your heavenly Father feeds them. Are you not much more valuable than they?" (Matthew 6:26). He is your deliverer.

Do You Want to Be Free?

I believe that many cases of incomplete ongoing deliverance exist because the person is afraid (perhaps unconsciously) of what he or she has buried in the darkness. The person is not ready to deal with it. Someone may be bargaining with God, wanting to be free only on his or her own terms. If that is your situation, pray for the grace to want *to want* to be free. Spend your time in the community of believers, receive the love and acceptance God has for you, and be changed by the truth. Keep a journal and pray through things with your friend or pastor, and keep busy doing creative things and serving others. Resist becoming introspective. One of the greatest needs in deliverance ministry is the proper context of faithful, loving relationships in which a person can be honest and accepted while responding to the process of transformation.

Sometimes the journey to freedom is slow, producing the desperation needed to embrace the truth that leads to freedom.

Do You Have Enough Faith?

Certain situations require more faith. Matthew 17:14–20 indicates that the disciples couldn't drive out a demon because they had "so little faith." But this is the context in which Jesus said that mustard-seed-sized faith can move mountains.

I like to think of faith as our grace-filled response to the revelation of God in Christ. If we lack faith, it is because we have not seen the greatness of God or have not responded to what He has revealed to us. There is no shortage of desire on God's part to reveal Himself to us. Faith increases when we act on what has been revealed to us.

How do you move mountains with mustard-seed-sized faith? *You have to act on it.* You have to speak it. As we act on our faith, we develop a history of the mighty deeds of God in our lives. Do you have enough faith? Of course you do! As a believer you just have to learn to act on it. As you do, build a history that you can stand on. If you are praying for deliverance for the first time, you have to rely on the history of God's action in other areas of your life or in the testimony of others. As you act, you will continue to build your history of the mighty acts of God.

God Can Do It Any Way He Wants

"When evening came, many who were demon-possessed were brought to him, and he drove out the spirits with a word and healed all the sick" (Matthew 8:16).

Learning about the principles of deliverance is very important. That is how we learn to cooperate with the Lord and assist others as they seek to receive their blessing. If we understand what is involved, we will be less likely to be deceived. When Monica told me that fear was still there, I knew something had yet to be uncovered. Experience and knowledge kept me from being tempted to fall into some past mistakes.

But we need to consider that Jesus can set His people free any way He wishes. He drove spirits out with a word. Sometimes He asked probing questions—what I call an "interview"—and other times He did not. Encountering Jesus can produce an instantaneous repentance that exposes the enemy and his lies and also brings deep conviction and blessing.

Paul, a high school student, was a very popular "partyer." Many students had shared with him about Jesus. It seemed as though he had clearly rejected the Gospel. Then Paul had a skiing accident and was in a coma for three days. The students prayed for him, fearing for his salvation. His youth leader was there when he came out of the coma. In a weak voice Paul said, "I saw Him; He is so beautiful. I wanted to stay. But He told me He is giving me a second chance." He had met the Lord! How incredible! We cannot limit God. The revelation of Jesus can do it all in a moment. We can cry out to God, asking that He set us free. Sometimes He just does it. Most of the time He takes us through a long journey. In doing so He teaches us much more about the spiritual life and how we can become His instruments for others.

THE POWER OF TEPEZCOHUITE

("TEP-EZ-CO-HEETY")

LOOKING FOR AN ORGANIC WAY TO TREAT SKIN CONDITIONS?

Mayan Magic Healing Balm speeds up the healing process with **Tepezcohuite**, its key active ingredient. In 1984, the Mexican Red Cross successfully treated severely burnt victims with **Tepezcohuite** following a series of gas station explosions near Mexico City.

Tepezcohuite not only protects the skin from the damaging effects of the environment, it also **relieves pain, heals without scarring, regenerates skin cells, and fights bacteria, viruses and fungi.** It is also a **non-toxic antibacterial agent** 300% more effective than streptomycin (Univ of Ottawa).

For serious, safe skin care, use Mayan Magic Healing Balm.

- 100% Satisfaction Guarantee
- Paraben Free
- Fragrance Free
- Not Tested on Animals
- Organic Extracts

PSORIASIS ? ECZEMA ? DRY SKIN ?
THE LAST CREAM YOU'LL EVER NEED

Mayan Magic contains a high percentage of **Tepezcohuite** - a tree bark extract, which has been used as an indigenous healer in Mexico for many years. Tepezcohuite is, among other fantastic healing properties, a <u>natural analgesic</u>, a <u>skin cell regenerator</u>, and is <u>anti-bacterial</u>.

The balm's **Shea Butter** base makes it a beautiful, creamy texture that absorbs into the skin well, without any oily residue.

Our customers raved about the results after using **Mayan Magic** on many skin conditions, including:

- Psoriasis
- Eczema (kids too!)
- Severe dry skin
- Cracked skin
- Rosacea
- Athlete's foot

- Superficial cuts
- Burns (including sunburns)
- Surgical incisions
- Tattoo aftercare
- Scars
- Diaper rash & more

Mayan Magic is also scent-free, paraben-free and is 100% satisfaction guaranteed.

Canadian Made

www.lavigneorganics.com

Then Jesus came to them and said, "All authority in heaven and on earth has been given to me. Therefore go and make disciples of all nations, baptizing them in the name of the Father and of the Son and of the Holy Spirit, and teaching them to obey everything I have commanded you. And surely I am with you always, to the very end of the age."

Matthew 28:18–20

Lord Jesus Christ, I thank You for the gift of faith that enables me to know You are with me even now. All authority in heaven and earth is Yours. I have nothing to fear. In the name of Jesus, I command every evil spirit I have renounced, every spirit behind the sins I have confessed, to leave me. Now! Thank You, Jesus, for setting me free from the influence of evil spirits. Thank You, Father, for sending Your Son to save me.

Then I heard a loud voice in heaven say: "Now have come the salvation and the power and the kingdom of our God, and the authority of his Christ. For the accuser of our brothers, who accuses them before our God day and night, has been hurled down."

Revelation 12:10

No longer struggling under the influence of the kingdom of darkness, we need to come fully into our inheritance as sons and daughters of God. The next chapter will help you to receive the blessing God has for you.

109

7

I Receive Blessing in the Name of Jesus

What matters supremely, therefore, is not, in the last analysis, the fact that I know God but the larger fact which underlies it—the fact that he knows me. I am graven on the palms of his hands. I am never out of his mind. All my knowledge of him depends on his sustained initiative in knowing me . . . there is no moment when his eye is off me, or his attention distracted from me, and no moment, therefore, when his care falters.

J. I. Packer[1]

Discovering Your Identity

"Oh, I remember everything that happened. That was the first time in my life that I had experienced God as my Father. I had never known His love before."

I had not seen Barbara for a year, and I asked if she could write down an account of what had happened when we prayed together. To my surprise her memory of what happened was different from mine. I remembered how the power of the fortuneteller's words over her life had been broken. I remembered how she was delivered from fear. Yet her memory went immediately to the prayer of blessing at the end of our session, when the love of God transformed her life. I should not have been surprised. That is how it is. The one who gives birth and receives the gift forgets the struggles of giving birth, for the old is gone and the new has come. Barbara had discovered her identity.

At the heart of Satan's attack upon you is his attempt to rob you of your true identity and destiny. Satan will do anything he can to keep you from knowing God as Father, Son and Holy Spirit. In Barbara's loneliness and isolation, she sought answers in the spiritual world and opened herself up to the influence of evil spirits. The enemy's ultimate aim was to keep her from knowing who she was and entrusting herself to the Father's care. Yet as God reveals Himself to us, our identity is revealed. Once the works of the enemy were destroyed in Barbara, she experienced the blessing of God as her Father, which in turn revealed her true identity. God revealed Himself and His love to Barbara in a very special way.

God Wants Us to Receive His Blessing

Jesus received special blessings of His identity and destiny at His conception, during His time in the womb, at His birth, through His circumcision/dedication, at His baptism and at the major points in His life, prior to going to the cross. Similarly, God desires our parents, the church and even society to be a channel of His blessing and protection to us. But we know that none of us was blessed as Jesus was. Some of us were neglected or even abused. Some of us were conceived at a very hard time in our family. As a result we have walked in fear, never finding a place where we really know we belong. Instances of divorce, violence and alcoholism have left many like beggars, seeking to find their blessing somewhere. We don't know who we are or where we are going. We do not know how significant we are or what is the meaning of our life. Perhaps the saddest part of it all is that we do not realize that God is holding our blessing for us. In the last four chapters, I discussed keys to unlocking the door to freedom in Christ. Once those four doors are open, we are in a position to receive what God most wants to give us.

At every major point of your life, when you needed to be blessed, God was there to bless you. Yet perhaps a cloud covered you and you were unable to receive the blessing. Perhaps it was like the seed on the path in the parable of the sower (Matthew 13:4). God blessed you, but other circumstances came and quickly robbed you; the blessing did not take root in your heart. You don't remember the blessing, only the pain.

Actually, God intended family life, patterns of prayer and the sacraments to serve as walls of protection against the enemy and to be a source of blessing to us. But many of the protective walls have been torn down, and we can look at our lives and see the effects of the thief, who has come to "rob and steal."

For those who have surrendered to the love of God in Christ Jesus, the old is gone, the new has come. Through faith and baptism, we have died and now we live for Him. Our identity is found in Jesus. We have a place before the Father because Jesus, the only begotten Son, lives in us, making us eternally the sons and daughters of God. Every act of God is eternal. The words and the works of Jesus are eternal. The Father's blessing of Jesus is eternal. As we find our identity in Jesus, we receive the very blessings that He received from the Father when He took on humanity. Just as Mary was an instrument of that blessing to Jesus, speaking to Him the things she treasured in her heart, so the Church, the "body of Jesus," is meant to be an instrument of the blessing that is ours in Christ.

Ask for Blessing

One woman we prayed for said that Janet and I wanted her to be free more than she did. I think of that honest response in terms of God and us: The good news is that God wants to bless you much more than you desire to be blessed. Allow yourself to receive from Him.

Bruce Wilkinson wrote a little book called *The Prayer of Jabez*. It seems as if everyone I know has read it. The message has released a fresh excitement about how much God wants to bless us and how delighted He is when we ask for more.

> Jabez called on the God of Israel saying, "Oh, that You would bless me indeed, and enlarge my territory, that Your hand would be with me, and that You would keep me from evil, that I may not cause pain!" So God granted him what he requested."
>
> 1 Chronicles 4:9–10 NKJV

Wilkinson exhorts us to ask for God's blessing: "When we ask for God's blessing, we're not asking for more of what we could get for ourselves. We are crying out for the wonderful, unlimited goodness that only God has the power to know about or give us." He explains that when you ask to be blessed "you're praying for exactly what God desires. Suddenly the unhindered forces of heaven can begin to accomplish God's perfect will—through you."

Prophetic Blessing

God's blessing sometimes comes through a prophetic word. The New Testament tells us that the gift of prophecy is meant for encouragement. Most people would seek the gift if they understood how much Jesus wants to bless His people by the power of the Spirit. He wants to speak His word into our hearts and affirm our identity in Him.

Such prophetic blessing involves two basic things. One is the awareness that it is God who speaks. In each example below, the person knew it was God. Second, prophetic blessing speaks deep into a person's heart. God knows my name. He knows who I am; He understands me like no other. Encouragement comes because God speaks to the meaning and purpose of my life.

Following a prophetic blessing, one woman moved me deeply as she declared, "Now I know that He knows me."

God Revealing His Love and Kingdom

At the end of one of our conferences, a man shared the following testimony.

"Before I came to the conference I asked my father to call me 'son,' which he did. I had asked him before to call me 'son,' and he would say, 'I am not that way, it is not comfortable for me. I prefer "my child."' But this was important to me. So I asked one more time. Then when I came to the front the other night to ask for God to bless me, a man came and laid his hands on my head. After a brief silence he said, 'My son.' He paused again and said, 'My son,' then again slowly and deliberately, 'My son,' and again and again he repeated the words 'My son.' These words penetrated deep into my soul. I knew God was speaking to me and filling the empty places in my heart as He revealed to me that He was my Father and I was His son."

In another part of the room, at the same time, a young man who came forward to be blessed began to weep. He had loved to play soccer and had great success on the field. He had the approval of many. Yet he carried a deep wound in his heart because his father never came to his games. He hadn't fully received his father's love and acceptance. When he came forward to be blessed, a man he never met said, "I have a picture of you playing sports, and even though your dad may not have been there, your Father in heaven wants you to know that He was there. He was at every game and He watched you with pride. He was not embarrassed to shout for you with pride so that everyone would know you were His son. His eyes were only on you. It is as if He were shouting in front of everyone, 'This is My son; look at My son!' The Father loves you." The young man's tears flowed as God healed his heart.

Later in the conference, I began to pray for a young priest. An image came to my mind, which I described to him. "I see a boy on a road. You have been on the road a long time. You have often felt alone on the road. But God was always there. He was ahead of you, calling your name, drawing you toward Him. You walked by faith because you couldn't always hear His voice. As you walk the road, it grows wider and wider. As it grows wider I see many spiritual children. The road leads right to the Kingdom of God. I think God wants you to know that you will have many spiritual children with whom you will share eternity."

He told me later, "I was greatly encouraged by your words, and it is true I have many spiritual children. I knew the picture was from the Lord, because I often struggle with a fear that I will not be faithful. It spoke to my heart."

God Knowing Me Personally

At a young age I came to realize the power of a personal encounter. When I was four I believed in Santa Claus. I did not understand how there was a Santa at the bank and another on the street corner and another at the department store. I was told that all of these were Santa's helpers. The one and only Santa was to be found in New York City at Altman's Department Store. The day came for my sister and me to take the train into the city with my father. After we went with him to his office, we were going to see the one and only

Santa Claus. As we turned the corner we could see him way up on a platform on the biggest chair I had ever seen. He looked exactly as I had pictured him. Before we got near the line, he looked across the room at us and said, "Neal and Rita, come right up here." He had a place for us on his lap. I don't remember anything else except coming home and saying, "Mom! Santa knew my name!" Years later I realized that my dad had set it up. But now I know something much better. The almighty God, the Creator of the whole universe, the One who set the stars in the sky and can count every dust mite in my mattress, knows my name.

One such personal encounter with God occurred in 1971. I was visiting the Word of God community in Ann Arbor, Michigan. Hundreds of people were coming to Jesus and being filled with the Spirit. I had come there to learn and to receive, but most of all I needed to know God's will for my life. At one point it was announced, "Following the meeting, our guest speaker will be in the prayer room for anyone who wants prayer." Mentally I prepared my list of needs for prayer, narrowing it down to three specific concerns.

Leeland Davis, a guest speaker known for his prophetic ministry, and two nationally known leaders came and sat in the circle waiting for the prayer session to begin. Not knowing exactly what happens in a prayer room, and realizing I couldn't hide in a circle of twenty people, I went over my list a couple more times. I didn't want to go blank if I was asked to share in front of these highly respected men.

Pastor Davis spoke to a man about his drug problem as if he knew him, exhorting him to break with sin and follow the Lord. Then he spoke to another and another. It was as if he knew each of them. Next he spoke words of encouragement and warning to one of the community's leaders.

As he finished this he peered over his half-sized reading glasses at me. "Three times the Lord has drawn me to look at you," he said. "There is a great anointing on your life. God wants to use you to bring good news to many." He spoke words of encouragement that specifically addressed each issue I had listed in my mind. "But there is great fear in your life," he said, and then he prayed for me to be set free. I received the blessing I was seeking on my trip to Michigan. There was no deliverance from my deeper fears that day. I did not receive direction for the next steps for my life. What I received was hope.

The hope that was born that day came from the understanding that God had spoken to me. This was not general encouragement; it was specific and it came from God. I knew as Pastor Davis spoke that God knew me. He spoke to my three mental petitions. It was God. He knew my name. He knew me. He addressed things deep inside, things I always knew but had no words to express. I wasn't embarrassed to hear about the fear in my life; I was relieved. God had a special plan for my life, and the name of my enemy was fear. The Lord was with me, walking me into the blessing described in Jeremiah 29:11: "'For I know the plans I have for you,' declares the LORD, 'plans to prosper you and not to harm you, plans to give you hope and a future.'"

To bless with such power is to empower someone for life's journey. God through His servant blessed me. I received something that we all need. I was affirmed in my identity and destiny.

It is nice when someone says nice things about you. But blessing comes when you are empowered by words that bring life and help answer the burning questions inside us all: "Who am I?" and "What is the meaning of my life?"

Your Name Is Important

In the Scriptures a personal name speaks to one's identity and destiny. Abram, which means "father of many," had his name changed as God revealed his destiny. He would now be called Abraham, which means "father of nations." Simon would be called Peter, which means "rock." The name Jacob literally means "to grasp the heel"; this represents Jacob's struggle to overcome among men. God changed Jacob's name when he wrestled with the Lord begging to be blessed. His name became Israel, which means "he struggles with God," pointing to the source of blessing for his life and the people of God that would be known as Israel.

Names are very important. We prayed before we named our children. Each of their names has a special meaning to us. On every birthday we would tell the story of their names' meaning. Now when I pray for them to be blessed, the meaning of their names often comes to mind because the meaning speaks to who they are. God sent an angel to make sure His Son was named Jesus, which means "the Lord saves." In some cultures children are not named until after they are born, which makes some sense, as the name has to do with a person's identity.

In Isaiah 43:1 God addresses His people: "Fear not, for I have redeemed you; I have summoned you by name, you are mine." God has assigned meaning and purpose to your name. It represents you. He loves your name. He loves to speak it. He knew your name before you were born, even before your parents spoke it. There is meaning to your name, and your life gives your name meaning. Let God speak your name to you. Reflect on the meaning of your name. Consider who God formed you to be "as he knit [you] together in your mother's womb" (Psalm 139:13).

Even if we have experienced prophetic blessing, it does not happen that often. What we need to know most is that God wants to speak to us regularly about our identity in Him. And if we ask Him, He will speak.

Read and listen to His voice in Psalm 139:11–18, written by King David:

> If I say, "Surely the darkness will hide me and the light become night around me," even the darkness will not be dark to you;

the night will shine like the day, for darkness is as light to you. For you created my inmost being; you knit me together in my mother's womb. I praise you because I am fearfully and wonderfully made; your works are wonderful, I know that full well. My frame was not hidden from you when I was made in the secret place. When I was woven together in the depths of the earth, your eyes saw my unformed body. All the days ordained for me were written in your book before one of them came to be. How precious to me are your thoughts, O God! How vast is the sum of them! Were I to count them, they would outnumber the grains of sand. When I awake, I am still with you.

Empowered for Life's Journey

Thirty years ago, when I was going through a difficult time, I asked someone to pray for me. I had committed myself to the Lord, and then the girl I had dated for four years decided it was not going to work; she found someone else. The man praying, who did not know me, began with a declaration: "God can mend a broken heart." With that, God got my attention. I have never forgotten the words that followed, a biblical phrase that was an admonition as well as direction and confirmation of God's blessing in my current pain: "He who places his hand to the plow and looks back is not worthy of me." I was to let the past go and move ahead with confidence. Thirty years later I still have my hand on the plow.

God wants to break into our lives and reveal that He is our Father. He wants to affirm our identity and destiny. We need to be blessed in order to succeed in life. Blessing is bread we need for our life's journey.

At that time Jesus came from Nazareth in Galilee and was baptized by John in the Jordan. As Jesus was coming up out of the water, he saw heaven being torn open and the Spirit

119

descending on him like a dove. And a voice came from heaven:
"You are my Son, whom I love; with you I am well pleased."

Mark 1:9–11

---

*My Father, thank You for sending Jesus and showing me the way
home to You. I have opened myself to You. My life is hidden in
Christ. Please bless my life. As I identify with Christ, I, too, can
hear Your words spoken over me: "You are my son/daughter,
whom I love: with you I am well pleased." In Christ I receive this
blessing—and every spiritual blessing You have for me. Thank
You, Father, for knitting me together in my mother's womb, for
calling me by name and for having a special plan for my future.
Your works are wonderful!*

For we are God's workmanship, created in Christ Jesus to do
good works, which God prepared in advance for us to do.

Ephesians 2:10

In the next chapter we will discuss ways to unlock freedom
at ever deeper levels as we continue to look to God for grace
and knowledge.

8

Staying Free and Going Deeper

Whenever you feel guilty, even if it is because you have consciously committed a sin, a serious sin, something you have kept doing many times, never let the devil deceive you by allowing him to discourage you. My beloved, may every fall . . . always become for us a small step toward a higher degree of perfection.

Maximilian Kolbe

Changes Need to Follow Deliverance Prayer

If we want to walk in freedom and blessing, there needs to be a change in the way we think and live, a change that builds on the gift of freedom we have been given. Not everyone makes that change.

Looking straight into his eyes I challenged Derrick with this question: "Do you want to be free?"

"Yes," he responded firmly.

"Then say, 'In the name of Jesus I renounce lust.'" His face began to twist as he rose from his chair, moving away from me. I was holding his hand and rose with him, repeating calmly and firmly, "If you want to be free, renounce lust." He wanted to but could not get the words out. "You can say it, 'I renounce lust.'" Finally he said it. I commanded the spirit to go and great relief came over the man. We gave him follow-up instruction and warnings and sent him on his way.

Derrick had come because he was having trouble staying faithful to his wife. Once before he had fallen and now he was dangerously close to falling again. In the interview we found out he had never known his father. When he reached puberty, his identity as a man came from the streets. He felt most like a man when he was conquering women and using them for his pleasure. He had made a Christian commitment and later married. His pastor asked me to come and pray with him, and he was delivered of deep hatred and lust. What a great victory that day!

But what a big disappointment months later when I found out he did not walk in his freedom and is now separated from his wife. Derrick never made the changes necessary in his life so that he could find spiritual support in the body of Christ. Without making changes, he simply reverted to his old ways.

Remember, Satan Is a Thief and a Liar

Jesus used a seed-planting metaphor to tell us there are several ways to lose the word of truth planted in our hearts: Some seed thrown on a path is eaten by birds; some thrown onto rocks doesn't have enough soil and therefore withers without roots. Other seed falls among thorns, which choke out the plants. And some seed falls on good soil and produces a large crop. Jesus explains the meaning of the parable:

> When anyone hears the message about the kingdom and does not understand it, the evil one comes and snatches away what was sown in his heart. This is the seed sown along the path.

The one who received the seed that fell on rocky places is the man who hears the word and at once receives it with joy. But since he has no root, he lasts only a short time. When trouble or persecution comes because of the word, he quickly falls away. The one who received the seed that fell among the thorns is the man who hears the word, but the worries of this life and the deceitfulness of wealth choke it, making it unfruitful. But the one who received the seed that fell on good soil is the man who hears the word and understands it. He produces a crop, yielding a hundred, sixty or thirty times what was sown.

Matthew 13:18–23

We need to be aware of the ways the enemy deceives us and robs us of the gift of God, the ways he keeps the seed from the good soil. Perhaps Derrick did not understand the message of the Kingdom, so the gift was quickly snatched away. If Satan did not rob Derrick this way, he would surely have attempted other means to rob him. Trouble and confusion may have done it. If he could not steal the gift quickly, perhaps materialism and worries would make him unfruitful. We must seek to be good soil for the gift God gives us.

Lesson Points for Staying Free

I want to tell you Karl's story and then turn to some lesson points for staying free that I've gleaned from his journey and my ministry—even my own life.

God had worked through Karl to bring deliverance to other people, but in his own life the results did not last. When he was a young boy an older cousin sexually abused him. He became both fascinated and repulsed by the experience and confused about his sexual orientation. Thoughts such as, "Maybe I have always been like this," tormented him as he considered himself destined to be a homosexual. Memories of normal preadolescent experiences became fuel for the devil. Being sexually stimulated in the presence of men led to self-hatred: "I hate my life." His constant questioning—What do these attractions mean for my life?—opened the door to a deeper fixation.

The good news is that Karl's desperation led him to Jesus, and he found a new life. He had been hopeless about his future. Feeling trapped, he'd thought he would one day live a gay lifestyle, but he knew it would never make him feel whole. At that point he embraced the cross and was willing to suffer whatever the cost to follow Jesus. I had prayed for him once, and he was free for a short time, but then his temptations became more intense. The second time we prayed, I presumed we had gone deeper and he was free. He was not.

The following is based on an interview I had with him: "Learning about deliverance was really amazing. I saw some deep changes for people and some things really did change for me as well. There is nothing you taught me that I disagree with. The problem is with me. When you taught me the process of deliverance I began to have hope, thinking that what was wrong with my experience in the past was that I did not do it right. Then I began to read a lot of books on deliverance that gave me the impression that if I just discovered the root, everything could be healed. That led me to introspection, which was bad.

"I had already been through a similar cycle several times. It began with a deep spiritual experience, then I had certain expectations for what it would mean, only to find myself disappointed. I would look at what was wrong with my experience so I could have a better experience. I didn't want to take responsibility for my own life and get up and walk. When I ran out of new spiritual experiences, in my heart I resolved, 'It didn't work. There is no such thing as freedom in Christ, at least not for me.' I became cynical."

Karl could not tell me one thing I taught him that led him in a downward spiral of introspection, and he *could* tell me some things that I said that would have kept him from going this route. "Why didn't you come back and talk to me?" I asked.

"It was probably my pride," he said. Eventually he accepted his condition as a "thorn in [his] flesh" (2 Corinthians 12:7), and he is no longer seeking freedom in this area of his life.

For some time this left me in turmoil. Could I have better prepared him for the process of deliverance? I loved this man and wanted him free. But I've had to leave my turmoil at the foot of the cross, reminding myself that God is the deliverer, and apart from Him we can do nothing (John 15:5). There is a mystery to the work of grace and freedom. My friend belongs to the Lord, and his future is in God's hands.

On the positive side, Karl now has a better understanding about spiritual experiences. He is no longer looking for an experience that will remove his need for "fresh grace" every day. He knows he will always have to walk by faith and not by sight.

Here are my lesson points for staying free:

Winning a battle is not winning the war

Every time territory is taken for the Kingdom of God you will have to hold it, defend it. It may be a day, a week, six months, but you will have to hold it. Land mines buried under the surface may explode. Snipers may take shots at you when you're not expecting it. There may be an all-out assault. Can you imagine what would happen if a troop of untrained volunteers, through a series of unusual circumstances, won a major battle in a war? War would be misrepresented to them. They would become proud, thinking it was their skill that won the battle. They would be set up for a fall. If a victory comes too easily, we can be deceived into thinking it will always be easy. And it's not.

Introspection is destructive

Prayer for inner healing is asking the Lord to release His love into an area of our lives that has previously been closed. In the prayer model I present in this book, inner healing often takes place in response to declarations of forgiveness, or spontaneously after a spirit has been cast out. Prayer for healing of the inner person is specifically addressed in the time of blessing, when the person's identity and destiny are affirmed. This type of prayer, along with the support of loving relationships, may be vital to strengthen the person so he or she is able to ask for more help. At other times the interplay between healing and deliverance is integrated, as it was for Kevin (whose story is found in chapter 15).

Introspection, by contrast, is self-focused—a desire to help oneself. It places me, rather than Jesus Christ, at the center. Karl's story is a perfect example of how Satan uses introspection as a tool to rob us of walking in true freedom.

I received a deep inner healing almost thirty years ago that influenced my life significantly. Soon I began to face more issues in my life that God was uncovering. But then I began to search out roots of thought or behavior patterns that related to my issues. It was not long before I became super-depressed. I had no one to help me and my efforts were misguided. I had to turn away from my introspection and set my eyes on Jesus.

The context of deliverance is the advancement of the Kingdom of God. Jesus is the captain and we are His servants. As we pursue Him, He will take initiative in our lives. We simply need to know what to do when issues rise to our consciousness. We need to know how to cooperate with Him. We would all do well to have a mature friend, a small group, a pastor or a counselor to pray with us and help us understand how to respond to what is going on within. Develop a relationship with someone you can talk to and pray with, and then go about your life loving and serving Jesus.

When some problem or destructive pattern comes up, bring it to Jesus, and then to your friend or pastor. A good protection against introspection and self-pity is to talk out loud to Jesus rather than just think about it. Talking to Him keeps it in perspective. Sometimes it is better to talk to Jesus in the presence of your friend than to talk to your friend about the problem. Often when I feel something is not right in a conversation, I stop it and have the person tell Jesus about it. It drives away self-pity, self-justification, blame casting and any wrong kind of dependency on me. It quickly exposes whether the person is looking for attention or really seeking Jesus.

Pride is our biggest enemy

Unfortunately pride is only exposed through our blunders. Karl admitted that his pride kept him from talking to me.

And I know the problem. I've suffered a great deal in my life due to my stubborn pride. It seems that God is very willing to let someone He loves dearly go through difficult times, sometimes for a long while, to strip away the pride His servants try to carry into battle. I am sure of this: I am much more concerned about the consequences of pride than I am about the devil's attack on my life. The devil can do nothing to me that God does not permit. The only power the devil has is the power we give (gave) him. The door was opened to his influence through the sin of our first parents, and we also give him power through our sin.

Deliverance takes place in the broader context of advancing God's Kingdom

Deliverance is much broader than deliverance from evil spirits. Once a person has a powerful experience of the Lord, the devil immediately sets that person up for a fall. When we encounter the Lord powerfully, we experience a taste of the coming Kingdom of God, where every tear will be wiped away. A sense of security and peace pervades us. When someone encounters the Lord, or goes through a significant healing, deliverance or deeper conversion, it is not unusual for them to think, "My problems are over." If mature believers do not provide support, the person may experience a big disappointment. Reading a book like this could lead someone to think, "Now I have the answer. Now I know what I need. I will get it right this time." We look for a formula for freedom instead of looking for a relationship. We want to escape the need to depend on the Lord daily. We want to be free, not from bondage but from facing the cross.

Deliverance from evil spirits removes the obstacles to freedom, the hindrances and the bondage. It does not remove the cross from our lives. Suffering is the pathway to maturity. The eradication of pain is one of our idols in the Western world. But suffering is part of what it means to be human. Maturity means being faithful even if we don't feel good, knowing there is trouble in this life and counting it all joy (James 1:2).

In deliverance we embrace the gift; we have been transferred, through the power of the death and resurrection of Jesus, from the kingdom of darkness into the Kingdom of the beloved Son. There is no way to avoid the cross by which we share in His suffering. In chapter 7, I quoted from Isaiah 43:1: "Fear not, for I have redeemed you; I have summoned you by name, you are mine." That verse is followed by a promise of God's presence in and through troubles, not necessarily an absence of troubles: "When you pass through the waters I will be with you; and through the rivers, they shall not overwhelm you; when you walk through fire you shall not be burned, and the flame shall not consume you."

Deliverance is an ongoing process

Unfortunately deliverance is often associated with peak experiences, even though peak experiences do not occur often. Deliverance should be an ongoing part of the process of conversion, as we pursue the Lord and surrender more of our lives to Him. Repentance, forgiveness, renunciation, authority and blessing are all part of our inheritance as sons and daughters of God.

The Ever-Deepening Freedom: Janet's Story

As we are working with God to "stay free," God Himself allows us to become free at ever deeper levels. This is illustrated well in the life of my wife, Janet.

For years Janet regularly had migraine headaches. The pattern was hard to figure out. Sometimes they'd occur the day we arrived at our vacation spot, and she would end up in bed for a couple of days. Other times she'd get one right before a spiritual event, such as a conference. Still other times one came before a family gathering like Thanksgiving. There seemed to be a connection to stress but nothing we could pinpoint. At any moment she could be robbed of a day or two of her busy life.

In 1996 we attended a conference on deliverance training. After the first talk Janet began to see the lights before her eyes, the sign that a migraine was coming. Immediately we prayed. Janet was determined to stay, but a half-hour later she decided she couldn't. She would need to go home. On her way to find me, she ran into a man who had taken this seminar already.

He said, "Let's pray one more time." After a minute he asked, "How long have you had these migraines?"

"Fifteen years."

"What happened fifteen years ago?"

"My mother-in-law was staying with us and went to the hospital with a very bad headache; she almost died from meningitis."

The man discerned that fear had tightened its grip on Janet at that moment of her life. When she renounced fear, she doubled over and wept tears of release. When she came up she believed she was healed. In uncharacteristic boldness she came to me declaring she was healed, and for a time she was totally free.

Seven weeks later, as we began an international event in Philadelphia called "30 Days of Gathering Around Jesus," she got her first migraine. She was really upset, feeling that maybe nothing had happened before. "Perhaps I made it all up," she thought.

Good friends of ours prayed with her. They encouraged her to claim her freedom and believe it. Janet resisted the idea, for too often she had been told by people to "name and claim" her healing. She had been told many times that you just have to believe you're healed and walk in it. This placed the burden on her and not on God. The advice always left her disturbed.

But this time was different. God had done something, so every time she felt the symptoms of a migraine coming on, she learned to pray with authority and not yield to the headache. As she grew in her ability to resist, she recalled that five years earlier a prophetic man named Bob Jones had prayed with her, telling her she was going to be used in deliverance ministry. He said her gift was going to be helping people stay free once they had been set free. Janet was being trained. As is often the case, her struggles were opportunities to learn something that would be used to help others.

Often after she shared her testimony of being healed, she would get the beginnings of a headache. We quickly learned to pray each time, giving God the honor for healing Janet. God had taken back territory held by Satan, and Satan was not happy about it. He wanted it back. This time her "believing" she was free was based on something God had done.

God was going to take it deeper. The day before a mission trip, one of our sons asked to speak to Janet. "I don't feel loved and accepted by you," he began. "You always act as if you're right and I am wrong, as if you are better than I am." Janet was hurt. Though she thought he chose an inappropriate way to tell her, and that he was overstating things, she also recognized the truth. Years earlier the Lord had convicted her of a spirit of superiority. She thought it was dealt with, but obviously it was not. Exposing it hurt. She wept for a long time before she came to me.

I listened and then asked how this connected to her childhood memories. She spoke of rejection by her friends and the fights between her father and brothers that caused her to be afraid. We had prayed about these things years ago, and Janet wondered why this same old stuff was coming up again. (It is important to remember that she was not looking for it or becoming introspective in an unhealthy way. It was just surfacing again.)

This time we prayed through the deeper issues that had made a home for fear, and since then Janet has remained free of migraines. This prayer put the nails in the coffin for migraines. It was not the stress but the fear beneath the stress that caused the migraines—fear of being in situations that were out of control in ways similar to her childhood experience.

Taking Responsibility in the Next Generation

Patterns of thinking and the spirits associated with those patterns can be passed from one generation to the next. Gaining victory in our lives helps not only us but also those who come after us. Our breakthroughs are a source of blessing for others, especially our children.

Just as we have been blessed by our parents' virtues of faith, hope and love, and the fruit of the Spirit they have manifested, so we also have been subject to the influence of evil spirits in areas where our parents have been in bondage. Bondages to fear, depression, hopelessness, legalism or pride create an atmosphere in which children grow. Helpful insights may come as we trace areas of bondage back to our parents or even earlier generations. Breaking the power of evil spirits in these areas is not enough. We have to take full responsibility for how we react to these patterns—making a home for the enemy—and begin to live by Kingdom principles.

Like Janet, my son Joseph struggled with fear, and like her he had migraines. When we break free, the change in us opens a door for our loved ones. But Joseph's response to fear was very different from Janet's. He had to discover and overcome Satan's plan for his life. He wanted me to share what he learned so that others could learn about taking responsibility for the freedom we have in Christ.

Joseph, the fourth of four sons, is a prize. He was so good and sweet growing up that we were naive about what the enemy's plan for him might be. Because he always presented himself as "good," he learned how to act "good" even though his heart was moving away from the Lord and from us. We had no expectation that Joe would begin to roam at age thirteen.

In seventh grade Joseph started getting migraine headaches. Joe—who already had difficulty in school—stayed home a number of days, unable to attend class. I believe he set records for lateness and absences. We took him to specialist after specialist; we prayed for him. We knew Janet was set free from the headaches; we didn't understand why Joseph was not. We prayed for Joseph to be delivered from fear. In fact we prayed against fear of every kind. What we didn't know was that he was experimenting with alcohol and drugs. We didn't know that perhaps Joseph did not want to be free. We thought his mood swings had to do with puberty, sickness and social adjustments. We did not consider that alcohol and marijuana were part of the equation.

When Joe was in ninth grade we received a call from the police station. They were holding our son, who was drunk. That opened our eyes and marked the beginning of a turn for Joe. Several months later he committed his life to Jesus through a Young Life group. For six months he did not have another headache, and then he, too, had to learn to walk in his freedom. But it took years.

Driving Joseph to college for the start of his freshman year was a time of reflection. He shared the following perspective on his journey:

"In middle school I opened the door to the enemy by using headaches to escape. I wanted to hide out and sleep in my room and not have to deal with pressures at school and social situations. The headaches were real but I gave them power. Of course, at the time I did not understand this; I just lived it. I felt depressed and lonely, like no one understood me. Alcohol and marijuana was just another route of escape. When I met the Lord I didn't have to escape anymore. I entered a new world. I was delivered from my slavery. I was high on God; I was so in love with Him.

"As time passed I realized that the world was still here, and there were still sinful ways I wanted to live. I wanted to escape. Then the headaches began to come back.

"This is how it would go. I would stay up late or see something wrong on TV, and I would give in to my sinful nature. The next morning I would wake up with a headache because I didn't want to face my sin or myself. How could I go to school being looked at as a Christian when I knew I did not live up to that image? I didn't want to be a fake, and I didn't want to rely on God's mercy.

"In my pride I wanted to be good and not rely on God's mercy. When I fell, I thought of myself as such a sinner and kept myself from God. I was afraid to face who I really am and who God really is. I was afraid of the world, and who I was. I faced the challenges of life with timidity."

Joseph would renounce his fears and turn back to the Lord, and relief would come—for a season. Then he would fall back into old patterns again.

He needed to grow. He needed to go deeper in the revelation of his own soul and the revelation of God's love. God mercifully provided people who helped him at a time when parents are often the last to be asked for help.

Joe needed to learn to stop living the lie. He learned that:

1. He needed to physically go out and do something and deny the headache its power to depress him. He also needed to act in a manner that did not play into the "escape" mentality—go to school, do work, be responsible.
2. He needed to stop, pray and remember the truth. "I understand the lie. Now I have a choice. I renounce the lie."

"After doing all this, either my headache would be gone or I would just accept it," he says. "On my best days it just didn't matter if the headache remained or left. I did what I am supposed to do, and I felt good about it. I still get headaches, but a lot less often. The difference is that I go through the above process and hardly have to think about it. I feel like I am in the process of redirecting the pathway of thinking that opened me up to the problem to begin with."

The process of learning a new response applies to his whole life. Joe admits that the struggle helped him grow in his relationship with the Lord. Now he is grateful for what he went through, because he learned about himself and Satan's diversionary plan for his life. Joseph, like each of us, needs to take responsibility for his life. The fact that an evil spirit was holding him in bondage does not make him more or less responsible. The fact that it was something passed on through the generations does not make him more or less responsible. We all need to take responsibility for walking in freedom.

Lessons Learned from Joseph: Greater Victory

Jesus warned that if a spirit goes out of a person and comes back finding the house empty, he may bring other spirits, and the person will be worse off than before. That may be the case for someone like Derrick, who stopped repenting.

But when a person seeks to follow the Lord, every fall can become a greater victory. The process of falling and getting up again can bring greater conviction and seriousness about living a committed Christian life. It can bring deeper humility and acceptance of our dependence on God.

Often the problem of "falling" is in not having the support of others and the teaching necessary to walk in freedom. If Joseph had not had support at such a young age, I doubt he would be walking in freedom today. I am so grateful for the saints God provided to support him.

If the oppression returns, a person is likely to be confused and not able to think clearly. One woman I know stopped going to church after experiencing a fall. She felt as though she had failed, and so she gave up. Hopelessness and discouragement returned. Fortunately she had a friend who stood by her, and she is walking in freedom today. Her defeat turned into a victory, and she learned a deeper lesson. We all need a friend, someone who knows us and knows the truth; someone with whom we can be honest and with whom we can live in the light. If you do not have a friend like this, ask the Lord for one. Pastors and counselors often serve as a substitute for strong, Christ-centered friendships. It would be better if they were a support to these friendships and not a substitute.

Knowing Your Weakness

In areas where we have been delivered, we need to be strengthened. That area may remain a weakness by which we continually tap into God's strength. We need to resist old patterns of thoughts and response. We are transformed by the renewal of our minds (Romans 12:2). It is a gift to know your weakness and to have a clear understanding of Satan's plan for your life. As we are filled with the truth and the wonder of God, we are less likely to go back to our old unhealthy "friends" for comfort when we find ourselves in a lonely place.

Responsibility

Many people want to remain children. Before God we will always be children, dependent on Him and trusting in His care and provision. But as sons and daughters who have been joined to Christ, we stand in the authority He has given us. In Him we have everything we need to take responsibility for our lives.

The book of Revelation tells how the saints in heaven overcame Satan and received salvation:

> Then I heard a loud voice in heaven say: "Now have come the salvation and the power and the kingdom of our God, and the authority of his Christ. For the accuser of our brothers, who accuses them before our God day and night, has been hurled down. They overcame him by the blood of the Lamb and by the word of their testimony; they did not love their lives so much as to shrink from death."
>
> Revelation 12:10–11

They overcame Satan, the accuser, by the blood of the Lamb and by the word of their testimony. Their word was joined to the Lamb's sacrifice. They declared with their very lives what was true. They had to take responsibility for what they had been given. Each of us must do the same.

Live in the Freedom of God-Given Protection

To protect us, God has set in place healthy patterns of church life, family life, cultural practices, and laws and governments that uphold moral standards. Sometimes we simply neglect the gifts of God, taking these protections for granted and not availing ourselves of them. Sometimes we don't receive all that God has provided for us because renewal is desperately needed in the Church.

The situation in which we find ourselves is very much like that of Nehemiah when he returned to Jerusalem. He found the city walls torn down. Rebuilding walls is a dangerous, difficult and time-consuming task; the enemy may attack anytime during this vulnerable period. Nehemiah posted guards day and night; half his team worked while the other half watched. Those who carried materials for the building kept one hand on their weapons. Most troubling of all was that the enemies looked like themselves; the enemies were Jews who had remained in Jerusalem during the exile and intermarried. They had compromised the faith of Israel, intermingling it with idol worship. There is always something familiar and deceptive about our enemies. We need to be alert and watch. But it is most important that we keep a view for the long run. We are building patterns of life that will protect and bring safety to us and to our families.

We cannot rebuild the Church or society, but we can do our part by taking full responsibility for our lives. Each person needs a strategy for living under the blessing of God. To walk in freedom we need to change harmful behavior patterns, acknowledge our vulnerability to sin and dependence on God, and deepen our relationship with the Lord every day through prayer, Scripture study and service. Each of us needs to find supportive and healthy relationships in which we are free to acknowledge our weaknesses and be affirmed in who we are. As we resist the lies and grow in the knowledge of our true identity and destiny, we can have confidence that God is faithful.

> Being confident of this, that he who began a good work in you will carry it on to completion until the day of Christ Jesus.
>
> Philippians 1:6

Thy Kingdom come!

Therefore, my dear friends . . . continue to work out your salvation with fear and trembling, for it is God who works in you to will and to act according to his good purpose.

Philippians 2:12–13

Lord, thank You for the freedom You have given me. Help me to recognize quickly the devil's schemes to rob me of the gift. Help me to do what I need to do as I place my confidence in You, that You will bring to completion the work You began in me.

On him we have set our hope that he will continue to deliver us.

2 Corinthians 1:10

Now let us consider how we can give away the gift we have received.

9

Bread for a Friend

Those who have come into a genuine contact with Christ cannot keep Him for themselves, they must proclaim Him.

Pope John Paul II (World Mission Sunday 2001)

He Gave His Bread to Jesus

Day after day a young boy followed Jesus in the crowds. He always wiggled his way to a place in front. He saw the love in Jesus' eyes when He touched and healed people. He hoped that someday Jesus would touch him. He loved the stories Jesus told and how he felt so safe and free near Him.

He thought, "When I grow up I want to be like Jesus." He noticed the different personalities of the disciples. He especially liked Andrew, quieter than the others but always attentive to Jesus and His needs. He imagined himself being one of Jesus' disciples, just like Andrew.

One afternoon a crowd gathered to hear Jesus on the mountainside. The boy ran to the front, just in time to see Jesus scanning the crowd. He heard Jesus say to Philip, "Where shall we buy bread for these people to eat?" (John 6:5). In confused panic Philip said, "Eight months' wages would not buy enough bread for each one to have a bite!" (John 6:7). The boy had never heard a disciple answer Jesus that way. In silence Jesus just drew on the ground and waited. As the disciples slowly stepped back, the boy looked intently at the Master. If Jesus was silent like that, something important was about to happen.

In the silence the boy thought. *Give it to Jesus.* His heart pounded. *Give it to Jesus.* All I have is five loaves and a couple of fish. *Give it to Jesus.* He doesn't need my food, what good would it do? *Give it to Jesus.*

"Excuse me, Mr. Andrew, sir, but I have some food I want to give to Jesus."

Andrew looked at the boy. "Come with me." Together they walked up to Jesus, closer than the boy had ever been. He felt weak with fear and excitement. "Some think that this is the Messiah. . . ." His thoughts were interrupted as Jesus looked up. Andrew spoke, "Here is a boy with five small barley loaves and two small fish, but how far will they go among so many?" (John 6:9).

Jesus smiled at the boy, as if He'd been waiting for him, as if his bread and fish were the most wonderful gifts anyone could give.

Jesus and the boy sat down, looking over the thousands of people. Some pushed and shoved. Some seemed uncertain, as though they were carrying a long list of life's hurts, hoping they would not be disappointed again. Others excitedly declared, "This must be the one." As the boy looked at the people with Jesus, he felt a deep peace. Something was different. The people looked so beautiful in a new way.

Jesus then took the boy's lunch, thanked God for it and distributed it to the crowd of five thousand people. The boy began to cry, though he didn't know why. Much later in life, as he experienced the compassion of Jesus in his heart, he would understand the meaning of those tears.

When everyone had eaten, Jesus asked the disciples to gather up the leftovers. "So they gathered them and filled twelve baskets with the pieces of the five barley loaves left over by those who had eaten" (John 6:13). Jesus had satisfied them all—by His power transforming a boy's meager but willing gift.

This boy had some bread, which God used when he gave it away to Jesus. Maybe you feel God hasn't given you much—just enough sustenance for yourself. But maybe He's also implanted enough love in your heart for you to want to share it with others. If you give your "loaves and fishes" to Jesus, what do you think He might do with it? In short, He will transform it for the furtherance of His Kingdom. He can and will turn our humble gifts—even the scars of our painful wounds—into greater compassion for others.

One Who Learned to Give

"There is a girl I am working with—I think you may be able to help her," Melissa said.

I had known Melissa, a recent college graduate and leader of a high school outreach, for several years, but we had never spoken about deliverance prayer. "What is going on with her?" I asked.

"She made a commitment to Christ, but she's having a hard time being pure," Melissa said. "Now she has shared some of the deeper issues in her life with me, and I don't know what to do about it."

"Do you think she wants to be free?" I inquired.

"Yes!"

I probed deeper, "Do you think she is ready to be honest?"

"Yes."

"I think praying with her will benefit her, perhaps in a significant way. We would love to pray for her. We would like you to be there. Do you understand how we pray for people?"

"Yes, I think so, because of Jamie—do you remember her?" she asked. Melissa explained that whenever Jamie gave her testimony she always included how her life changed when we prayed for her. "Several months ago I was with Jamie, and she prayed for her friend Laura. She prayed the way you prayed with her, having her forgive and renounce things. I was very moved by the prayer and the results. Laura's relationship with her dad has greatly improved since they prayed. When the time came for Laura to return to the university for her sophomore year, her dad was unusually upset about her leaving. He said, 'Laura, I feel like I am just getting to know you.'"

Jamie had never been trained, nor had she received any teaching about praying with others for deliverance. But because she had gone through a non-threatening process that seemed normal, she instinctively understood what went on even though I never mentioned anything about evil spirits or deliverance to her. She had some bread to give her friends.

So Many Are Waiting for Help

Two years before, on a trip to Eastern Europe, Paul had been the last person on our list of people wanting prayer. But we had run out of time, needing to leave for the airport to catch our flight. On this return trip, we would make sure we had time with him.

Paul had been committed to the Lord for a number of years. He played the guitar and loved to lead others in the praise of God. He is a humble man filled with kindness and love. Prior to giving his life to Jesus, he had been in a rock band and regularly slept with different women several times a week. Through several of these women he had connections to the occult.

In marriage he was faithful and loving, yet he felt something was not quite right in his sexual relationship with his wife. Paul opened his heart to us and shared the many hurts and rejections he experienced prior to life in the rock band. We took him through the process outlined in this book. When we prayed, it seemed as though a great weight was taken off him. He took in deep breaths as if breathing fresh air for the first time.

Like many others, Paul had adjusted his life to accommodate the subtle whisper of guilt and condemnation from past events that had long been forgiven and buried in Christ. In recent years, as he immersed himself in the Word of God, listening to the voice of Christ, those whispers had grown fainter but had not been silenced. We now rejoiced with Paul as the entryway was exposed and shut and the power was broken.

But we left Paul and Eastern Europe with one question: Why in two years' time did Paul not find the help he needed? Why had no one helped to walk him through the release available in Christ? Why did he have to wait so long? Jesus expressed His heart for those who are waiting when He responded to criticism for healing on the Sabbath. "Then should not this woman, a daughter of Abraham, whom Satan has kept bound for eighteen long years, be set free on the Sabbath day from what bound her?" (Luke 13:10–16). Those who have been set free are often an instrument for others.

Who, Me?

When people tell me they feel inadequate to witness to and pray with others because they are too broken, I like to remind them of the biblical story of Mary Magdalene, from whom Jesus cast seven demons. From the day of her deliverance, she followed Jesus, living as a disciple. I sense that Mary was a woman who set her eyes on Jesus, and yet she never forgot what the pain of bondage felt like. As she gave her painful past to Jesus, she allowed Him to use it to soften her heart. Standing at the foot of the cross was a woman who could weep for her own loss and that of others. And she plays a key role in the resurrection story.

John's Easter account says she went to the tomb before dawn only to find the stone rolled away and the body gone. "How can this be?" she asked. In distress she ran to Peter and John and told them that "they" had taken away Jesus' body. Peter and John came, confirmed the empty tomb and left Mary alone again, weeping. Then she saw two angels, who asked her why she was crying. She again said "they" had taken away her Lord. Suddenly she turned around and saw Jesus, though she didn't recognize Him. He, whom she supposed to be the gardener, also asked why she was crying. Then Jesus called her by name: "Mary." In the moment He called her name, He revealed Himself and her heart opened to see the One she loved.

John 20 presents an extraordinary picture. The risen Jesus is about to return to the Father when He hears weeping and sees one searching for Him who is desperate to find Him, one whose heart has been broken. Out of love He chooses to go to her first. Jesus gives her a blessing—and a mission: "Do not hold on to me, for I have not yet returned to the Father. Go instead to my brothers and tell them, 'I am returning to my Father and your Father, to my God and your God'" (John 20:17).

What is the blessing? Jesus tells her He is returning to "my Father and your Father." That makes Mary His sister. She is part of His family. The mission? Mary, the one from whom seven demons were driven, is privileged to be the first to declare, "I have seen the Lord." Though she experienced great sin, she was the first to give witness to the risen Jesus, sharing the victory of Christ's Kingdom with her brothers.

Pain Transformed to Compassionate Ministry

Testimonies of healing and deliverance often tell only the end of the story, the time right before God reveals His love, touches and heals. These testimonies give hope to the afflicted but don't give much insight to the process by which God, over time, prepares someone to receive his or her liberty. When I pray for people, I am very aware that it has been their faith and their struggle to cooperate with His grace that has brought them to the brink of freedom.

In chapter 7 I told how God blessed me in 1971 through Pastor Davis, following a prayer meeting in Ann Arbor, Michigan. Pastor Davis spoke clear words of affirmation I had longed for, words of blessing. He also named and exposed one of my enemies, fear. I had lived with that fear since childhood, and it influenced my ability to express myself. I never raised my hand at school or volunteered an answer. I was labeled as shy, and I hated that term. I wanted to break out of my prison but spent most of my younger years trying to convince myself I was okay despite my limitations. In the meantime I looked for ways to avoid pain through drinking and parties.

In the months after Pastor Davis word of prophecy, I sought healing. I knew fear gripped my life but I didn't know where it came from or what I could do about it. "Heal me, Lord" became my constant prayer.

I asked my cousin, Fr. Mike Scanlan, to pray for me. (I was in my early twenties at the time.) Before doing so he asked a few questions. "Tell me about your relationships in your family growing up," he said.

"I had a very difficult time with Mom and my sister," I replied.

"What about your father?" he asked.

"I don't have any bad memories." I knew he was looking for old wounds that needed to be healed and forgiven. "I think I need to forgive my mom and my sister."

He prayed for me, but I didn't perceive a great change in my life.

In the months following the prayer, I sensed a great sadness welling up, as if the prayer had exposed a deep longing and emptiness. A pastor came for a weekend visit with the family I was staying with. All he could talk about was God as a Father. I didn't relate to God as Father, and that thought brought to mind the old negative message that something was wrong with me.

Foolishly, I protested inwardly that the Father was second best. I knew Jesus, and I knew the Holy Spirit as the Spirit of Jesus, and *He* was the way to the Father. What more did I need? I had received the Spirit of Jesus, hadn't I? I was trying to cover up what had been exposed. But it was too late. There it was: I did not know God the Father. What's more, it seemed that the root of my block lay in my relationship with my dad. I didn't have bad memories of him; I just didn't have enough memories. Alcohol kept him emotionally distant. Work kept him physically absent. His father had died when he was two years old, and he couldn't give me what he had not received.

Sadness and desperation led me to take a four-hour trip to see my cousin Mike and ask for prayer once again. This time he prayed that the love of God would fill every area of lack. As I received that love, Jesus showed me the Father and I received the Father's blessing. My self-perception of being an outcast in my family was exposed. God removed the lie and placed in me the truth that I was loved. A new ability to express myself, to talk, became evident to those around me. God's love is not just a concept but is practical and life changing.

God touched me and gave me a new ability to love others. He gave me what I could not have hoped for or expected. In Ephesians 4:8 we are told, "When he ascended on high, he led captives in his train and gave gifts to men." Jesus had set this captive free, and He gave me a gift. By the power of

His love in me I could love others. I could help others receive what I had been given.

Fifteen years later, at a conference led by John Wimber, this prayer for healing went deeper, to a prayer of deliverance. For years I had suspected I needed deliverance prayer. I had received many healings but knew I needed an even deeper touch of God's love.

On the last day I spoke to a man who had a deliverance ministry. He suggested we pray together. Sitting across a table from me, he asked the Lord to touch me. Then he said, "Do you feel that?" For the first time I recognized that something that was a part of me, part of my personality, was not really me.

Yes. This was something very familiar to me; it seemed like a companion I had known all my life. No longer hiding, it was now exposed as heaviness on my chest. This minister looked as if he were gazing into my soul and said, "What happened?"

My mind went to a school classroom: "Something happened in first grade."

"What happened in first grade?" Without any conscious memory I spoke what came to my mind.

"I was humiliated in front of the class." He encouraged me to forgive my teacher.

"In the name of Jesus, I forgive my teacher for humiliating me."

Then he said, "In the name of Jesus I command the spirit of rejection to leave." The weight that was on my chest lifted into my head and then left. I was free. With rejection left the fear of rejection. Now I knew my enemy's name, and I could resist the habits and patterns that had developed in me.

A season of grace followed. I had a new boldness as I prayed for others, and I saw many people delivered from the influence of evil spirits. I learned what it meant to weep with the Lord's compassion, to listen without judgment and to empathize without needing an answer. I also learned to point people toward Jesus, who is the answer for all of life's questions. I still had much more to learn and hurdles to overcome, but God was confirming what He did in me by what He was doing through me.

Children's Bread

To be blessed is to receive bread for life's journey. Those who have received such blessing are privileged to seek blessings for their friends.

I find great insight in a healing described in Mark 7. A non-Jewish woman, the mother of a demonized girl, fell at Jesus' feet and begged Him to drive the demon out of her daughter.

You can imagine this mother's pain, seeing her daughter in great distress, perhaps uncontrollable, manifesting signs of an evil presence. In motherly desperation she likely took her to many who promised help—only to be disappointed. Then she heard of Jesus, and she pressed in to the house He was visiting.

Knowing her real need, Jesus had an unusual response. "First let the children eat all they want," He told her, "for it is not right to take the children's bread and toss it to their dogs." Jesus referred to deliverance from evil spirits as the *children's bread*. It is something that belongs in a special way to the children of God. Even understanding that Jesus knew He was first sent to the children of the covenant, His response seems uncharacteristic and difficult to understand. A Jew might well have referred to the Gentiles as dogs, a term of contempt. This Gentile woman could easily have taken offense but didn't, most likely because of the tone of Jesus' voice and the look upon His face. He had raised the issue that would keep her from receiving grace and healing from the Jewish Messiah. But the desperation of her circumstance broke her pride.

What was her response? It was not an effort to save or defend herself, but to save her daughter. She humbled herself. "Yes, Lord," she replied, "but even the dogs under the table eat the children's crumbs." Then He told her, "For such a reply, you may go; the demon has left your daughter."

What a woman of faith! On someone else's behalf, she begged Jesus for deliverance. This woman was the intercessor her daughter needed.

Bread for the Journey

Receiving what we have long awaited may seem like the end of a journey. In fact it is only the beginning. Like Jamie, we can give because we have received. She was like the little boy who brought his fish to Jesus. She did not fully know the value of what she had received until she gave it away. Mary Magdalene pressed on until she encountered the Lord, the One she loved. Ultimately Jesus told her to go and tell others the good news she had received. She carried the testimony for the rest of her life: "I have seen the Lord." The journey begins again when we are touched by the compassion of the Lord. Then we become like the mother of the demonized girl. We can't stop knocking; we keep calling out until we have bread to give our family and friends. Deliverance is the children's bread. God wants to work through you to bring deliverance to those you love.

> If I speak in the tongues of men and of angels, but have not love, I am only a resounding gong or a clanging cymbal. If I have the gift of prophecy and can fathom all mysteries and all knowledge, and if I have a faith that can move mountains, but have not love, I am nothing. If I give all I possess to the poor and surrender my body to the flames, but have not love, I gain nothing.
>
> *1 Corinthians 13:1–3*

Father thank You for the many keys to freedom You have given me in Your Son. Your love has set me free. I want to be Your disciple, an instrument for Your love to others. Truly Your love flowing through me is my liberation, the final key. Lord, give me that gift of love.

Therefore love is the fulfillment of the law.

Romans 13:10

The next section explains how you can help a friend (or they can help you). It will provide a deeper understanding of the principles that you have encountered in reading and reflection. Perhaps you should first pause and pray through the last chapters, seeking God for the blessing you need.

PART 2

HELPING A FRIEND

10

Helping Others to Stretch

When people have been given an internal image and vision of
who they are and where they are going, then they can stretch
themselves to do the exploits of God.

Craig Hill[1]

Deliverance prayer should be restored to normal Church life[2];
it should not be restricted to those who experience major
bondage and blatant diabolical manifestations. Yet in many
parts of the Church there is no place for it. In a local newspaper I read an article entitled "It Was No Exorcism." It seems
that in 1996 an evil spirit troubled Mother Teresa while she
was in the hospital. The bishop sent a priest to her to "say
the prayer of exorcism." He "recited the prayer of exorcism
to drive out evil spirits," and it was reported that she slept
peacefully that night.[3]

Many church leaders have a place for exorcism for those
labeled "possessed" but no place for the simple prayer of
authority to drive away spirits troubling one of God's children. This seemed to be the case for Mother Teresa. It was

newsworthy because many are not used to dealing directly with evil spirits. My prayer is that we move toward a language and a place for deliverance to be exercised in the ongoing life of the church.

Building on the Foundation

In the first part of the book I imparted the basic principles of how to cooperate with Jesus as He sets the captives free. Let me summarize:

- Because of Jesus, there is hope and we can ask for the blessing we need.
- Jesus is our hope, our Savior.
- Jesus saves us from sin and from Satan's plan for our lives.
- Jesus reveals to us our hearts so that we can repent.
- Jesus gives us the power to forgive and to renounce the enemy in the areas in which he has gained influence.
- We have authority over the devil in the name of Jesus.
- God wants to bless us by revealing who we are so we might fulfill our destiny.

The road to that destiny involves both holding the territory and deepening the freedom we have been given. What is the gift? Compassionate self-giving. What we have received is what we must give. If you have encountered the truth of these principles, you have something to give. It is in our growing freedom that we find our gifts and our ability to serve. The process by which we are liberated gives us a testimony, a gift to give others. When the love of God is poured out into our hearts, when we have received the "children's bread" (Mark 27:7), we will pray for others to receive the same bread. Some of you will pray with friends and see them receive the blessing you received. For others of you, the door is being opened, as it was for me, to incorporate deliverance prayer in your ongoing service to the Lord. This part of the book will help you help others find their deliverance from evil spirits. Understanding the depths of your own soul and the process by which God has been liberating you[4] is the best preparation for this ministry.

First Things First

As I was stretching after my workout at the gym, I noticed a young trainer working with an elderly woman. "Lean against me, good, ten, nine, eight . . . you're doing great. Good, two, one." The trainer had tested the woman's flexibility and was now taking her through a number of stretching exercises. Some I had never seen before. Five minutes later he said, "Now let's see if you made some progress." The woman was astonished. She gained about ten inches as she reached toward her toes.

"You're amazing! Are you a wizard or something?" she asked, delighted.

"No. I didn't do it. You did it," the trainer responded. "You're the one who is amazing."

Helping someone get free of the influence of evil spirits is very much like this. We are helping people learn how to stretch out and touch Jesus, their deliverer. It may feel good if they express gratitude and admiration to you, but it may not be helpful in the long run. People are better served if they leave a prayer session knowing how to cooperate with Jesus in the deliverance process. Only Jesus saves and delivers us from evil spirits.

The apostle Paul knew this and made it clear to his readers: "For what I received I passed on to you as of *first importance*: that Christ died for our sins according to the Scriptures, that he was buried, that he was raised on the third day according to the Scriptures" (1 Corinthians 15:3–4, emphasis added).

Our hope for freedom rests on what Jesus has done on our behalf. It is His initiative to set the captive free. Jesus was not unclear about His mission. We are told that on one Sabbath day He went into the synagogue and stood up to read from the prophet Isaiah. He found a certain passage and read aloud: "The Spirit of the Lord is on me, because he has anointed me to preach good news to the poor. He has sent me to proclaim freedom for the prisoners and recovery of sight for the blind, to release the oppressed, to proclaim the year of the Lord's favor." He then said, "Today this scripture is fulfilled in your hearing" (Luke 4:17–21).

In Luke's gospel these are the first words of Jesus' public ministry. This was His mission statement and it still is. He continues His mission through the Church, through us.

As you pray with others for deliverance, keep in mind that the key players are Jesus and the person being prayed for. Deliverance models that focus on the minister may leave the person delivered of an evil spirit, but new problems will arise if he becomes overly dependent on the person praying for him or overly focused on demons. Just as the elderly woman learned how to take responsibility for the new level of flexibility in her body, each person is responsible for the level of liberty he is given. Their active participation should not be minimized. "I repent . . . I believe . . . I forgive . . . I renounce . . . I command. . . ." Learning the power of our declarations is part of the deliverance process. When we assist others in deliverance, we are helping them to take responsibility for their lives and to respond in faith to Jesus.

Principles and Models

In the first part of this book I communicated spiritual principles that relate to, but are not limited to, deliverance from evil spirits. They are basic principles for growing in freedom in the Christian life. These principles are exercised every day as we walk with the Lord. Being set free is part of our ongoing conversion. It is our inheritance.

To assist someone, we need a method to put the principles into practice. It is helpful to learn from others and avoid the mistakes they have made.

I have learned a great deal from others.[5] But I have learned the most by making mistakes and struggling to understand them. As you consider the model of deliverance prayer I present here, I welcome you to test it by the principles in part 1. A good student learns from his teacher, but eventually what he has learned will look a bit different.

Recently I investigated a program called City As Parish, where I gleaned the following wisdom: "If the method you use looks exactly like the one you were taught, it probably won't last. You need to struggle with material for something to become truly yours. If you implement what you have learned exactly as you were trained in it, you will eventually fail. If you struggle with it and tear it apart, it will look different. Then it will be yours."

Let God Teach You

Each of us needs to learn from others as a foundation, but most of all we need to let the Lord teach us.

The influence of evil in people's lives cannot be reduced to a formula. Understanding the principles is the basis for us to learn how to cooperate with the Savior.

After Jesus had a lengthy private conversation with the woman at the well, His disciples approached Him. John 4:27 tells us they "were surprised to find him talking with a woman. But no one asked, 'What do you want?' or 'Why are you talking with her?'"

A rabbi was not to speak to a woman in public, particularly a Samaritan woman. But seeing Jesus' great compassion, the disciples didn't question Him. They were left with something to ponder, something to wonder, something to learn. Some questions are not answered with words. The answers come over time. Some truths are far deeper than words and can only be perceived over time. Hearing the answer is not the same as finding the answer.

Your greatest opportunity to learn is as you love the person God sent to you for prayer. That is when you will learn what it is you have read and heard about. He is our teacher. The person He sent your way is perfectly picked so that you can be an instrument of God's love for them, but also so that you can be instructed. When God teaches us something, He gives us the opportunity to share what we have learned, to give away the Good News. As we do so, we learn. Not everyone is called to a ministry of deliverance,⁶ but all can be used to help a friend receive freedom.

When a friend comes for prayer, he is placing great trust in you. That means you have great responsibility. Your first responsibility is to love by listening deeply. What does your friend want? What is the Holy Spirit saying? Listen with empathy, seeking to understand without trying to "fix" his feelings. Are there any clues to how the enemy might be at work? Let the Lord fill you with His love for your friend.

When Janet and I minister deliverance, first we pray, asking Jesus to help the person. Next we help him respond to what has been revealed to him about the lack of freedom in his life. We help him express his faith through God-given repentance, forgiveness, renunciation, authority and blessing. If you listen with love and acceptance, your friend may share with you things he has never shared with anyone.

Part of your responsibility is to ensure the person's ability to decide what he is willing to release. His deliverance is between Jesus and him. You are just assisting. It is better for someone to make his own decision even if it is not a good one. Bad may be good in the long run. Some people want others to decide what they should do. Don't cave in to this request. Stand with him, teach him what you know and let him make decisions for himself.

Being prepared and ready to assist a friend is very important. Sometimes simply asking the Lord's help may initiate an encounter with God that sets the person free. On the other hand, the instruction and example we give may help the person enter into a lifelong process of transformation.

There are a number of complete handbooks on deliverance ministry. This is not one of them. My goal is to teach you the basics so you can proceed simply and safely. If it is not simple, you might never pray for anyone. If it is not safe, you may pray for one person and then quit.

Get started in the spirit of the prayer of Jabez, which says, "Oh, that You would bless me indeed, and enlarge my territory, that Your hand would be with me, and that You would keep me from evil, that I may not cause pain!" (1 Chronicles 4:9–10, NKJV).

Seek the Power of the Holy Spirit

"When Jesus had called the Twelve together, he gave them power and authority to drive out all demons and to cure diseases" (Luke 9:1). We should not presume to think that we can drive out demons unless we have received the power of the Holy Spirit.

Before His ascension Jesus told His disciples to wait for the spiritual power. This is evident in Luke 24:49, "I am going to send you what my Father has promised; but stay in the city until you have been clothed with power from on high," and in Acts 1:8, "But you will receive power when the Holy Spirit comes on you; and you will be my witnesses in Jerusalem, and in all Judea and Samaria, and to the ends of the earth."

Ask God to make you His instrument. Ask Him to give you the grace of surrender and to fill you with the Holy Spirit.

Are You Anointed for Ministry?

When God touches someone in a dramatic way, whether to heal or deliver from bondage, we witness signs and wonders that point to the clash between the kingdom of darkness and the Kingdom of God. Dramatic encounters may not be part of everyday experience, but the process of liberation should be common to the life of the believer. Jesus instructed all of us to pray for deliverance from the evil one (Matthew 6:13). Does it not follow that we should be prepared to help a friend? "Who me?" you might ask.

When the angel of the Lord appeared to Gideon and said, "The LORD is with you, mighty warrior," Gideon's response was basically, "Who me? Are you kidding?" He didn't perceive himself to be good enough or prepared enough to be God's anointed. "How can I save Israel? My clan is the weakest in Manasseh, and I am the least in my family" (Judges 6:15).

It is not pleasing to God when we unfavorably compare ourselves to others. God sees something in you that you do not see. He has appointed works for you to do, and in this sense you are anointed for service. Anointing, simply put, means "God is with you for a particular purpose." It may be in the area of deliverance prayer or another area. You may have to grow into your calling. In the following chapters I will give you a glimpse of how long my journey to this point in deliverance ministry has taken.

No matter how much anointing we experience, the bottom line is the same for all. What are we doing with His anointing? Have we learned to love? The power of God and the love of God are the same. Do we serve in the most loving way possible?

Deliverance from evil spirits is a normal part of the Christian life. In order for it to take its place in the life of the Church once again, the works of the devil need to be demystified, and we need to develop a language that reflects that reality.

Whenever the spirit from God came upon Saul, David would take his harp and play. Then relief would come to Saul; he would feel better, and the evil spirit would leave him.

1 Samuel 16:23

Father, teach me how to comfort others with the comfort I have received from You. You are the Father of compassion; release Your love in me and show me how I can give Your love away. Please use me to bring liberty to others. Show me how You want me to serve.

Praise be to the God and Father of our Lord Jesus Christ, the Father of compassion and the God of all comfort, who comforts us in all our troubles, so that we can comfort those in any trouble with the comfort we ourselves have received from God.

2 Corinthians 1:3–4

The enemy uses fear to hold us back from the purposes of God. Before we discuss "how not to" and "how to" assist others in their deliverance, we will take a look at overcoming unfounded fears associated with deliverance ministry in chapter 11.

11

Should I Be Afraid?

A good Christian watches continually, sword in hand, the
devil can do nothing against him, for he resists him like a
warrior in full armor; he does not fear him, because he has
rejected from his heart all that is impure.

John Mary Vianney

Born in Bradford, England, in 1859, Smith Wigglesworth
was a plumber known for his faith. The story is told that one
night he was awakened by a creaking sound in the downstairs
parlor. Wigglesworth took his candle and started down the
steps. The creaking grew louder. A foul, deathlike odor filled
his nostrils. As he approached the room where the sound came
from, he felt the air turn cold. Peering into the room, he saw
the source of the creaking: a figure in his rocking chair. As he
stepped closer, he saw that it was the devil himself! "Oh, it is
only you," Wigglesworth said as he blew out his candle.

That story stands in stark contrast with the fear of Satan
I sense these days. As I visited a former Communist bloc
country, I was told the only books available on deliverance
were books you would not want to read at night before you go

to bed. They produced fear, detailing nightmarish accounts of evil spirits manifesting themselves, much like the scenes associated with *The Exorcist*. They contain stories of spirits taking control over the individual, causing bizarre contortions, levitations and vomiting. The devil loves to produce fear in order to extinguish love. For as we are told that love casts out fear (1 John 4:18), fear drives away selfless acts of love.

On a recent flight to Haiti I felt tempted to fear the devil. As the island came into view, my thoughts flew to all the things I had heard about this country. It had been dedicated to Satan. The voodoo drums are played continually, especially directed against missionaries. "You're going to Haiti to teach about deliverance? Better you than me. You had better get a team of intercessors behind you." These were typical responses when people heard where we were going. Every once in a while I would catch myself thinking, "What are you doing, going to Haiti to teach on deliverance? You're getting in over your head." But as we approached the airport, I heard the Lord speak to me: "This is My country and My people. It does not belong to Satan. I plan to take it back. Don't believe the lie."

Fear Is Based on Lies

During a seminar on deliverance on a trip to Europe, one of our interpreters told me that two priests in his diocese had been involved in deliverance work. One was working against cults, and the other was doing exorcisms. Both disappeared. One leaped off a moving train and disappeared for six months. Now he is back—what happened to him nobody seems to know—but he is not doing exorcisms anymore. The other priest disappeared for six months, too, and they found him living with a man in a homosexual relationship. For about twenty seconds fear tried to grip me. "I am in over my head. The enemy must be especially strong here."

Then I caught myself. The thought came to me, "Fear is useless; what is needed is trust." Fear is the door to bondage. If Satan could plant fear in my heart, then with every negative thing that happened he could build a place to rest. Jesus said, "Get behind me, Satan!" (Matthew 16:23). I said the same.

"For God did not give us a spirit of timidity, but a spirit of power, of love and of self-discipline" (2 Timothy 1:7).

I heard a news report about a Catholic archbishop from Africa known for performing exorcisms who came under the influence of the Reverend Moon. He married a woman Moon had chosen for him. What is going on? Satan is discrediting the deliverance ministry and bringing fear. He is creating fear and caution in pastors. But Mark 16:17 says one of the signs that will follow believers is that they will cast out demons.

While we should not be afraid, I do give cautions, which I'll address further in the next chapter. I have been in prayer meetings where more "prayer" was directed toward the devil than toward God. And I have been at meetings where people who lacked wisdom and authority addressed the powers and principalities. Satan's power is real, and we can be subject to it if we are proud or operate outside the authority the Lord has given us. One person boasted about his work with the demonic and how it did not affect him, yet at that very time his marriage was falling apart.

Nothing Will Harm You

In Luke 20, we see Jesus sending out 72 disciples, giving them authority to overcome the power of the enemy. They came back rejoicing, "Lord, even the demons submit to us in your name." Jesus had a twofold response.

First, He told them that nothing would harm them, because He had given them authority over all the power of the enemy. "I saw Satan fall like lightning from heaven. I have given you authority to trample on snakes and scorpions and to overcome all the power of the enemy; nothing will harm you" (Luke 10:18–19). If they walked in what He taught them, and the authority He gave them, they had nothing to fear. This is not a trick statement. He said quite plainly, "Nothing will harm you." Jesus should know, as He "saw Satan fall like lightning from heaven."

Jesus said something else that was very important. "However, do not rejoice that the spirits submit to you, but rejoice that your names are written in heaven" (Luke 10:20).

When we see the Kingdom of God advancing, and territory being taken from the evil one, we are witnessing things that prophets and kings longed to see and hear but did not (see Luke 10:24). It seems to me that it would be quite natural to rejoice. As a matter of fact Jesus rejoiced over their report. Verse 21 says,

> At that time Jesus, full of joy through the Holy Spirit, said, "I praise you, Father, Lord of heaven and earth, because you have hidden these things from the wise and learned, and revealed them to little children. Yes, Father, for this was your good pleasure."

Jesus said to rejoice, but not because spirits submit to you. When I was younger a subtle pride arose in me as I realized that demons responded when I spoke the name of Jesus. Now I am keenly aware that what happens in deliverance is the work of Jesus; I am just His instrument. I never even think about spirits submitting to me. I rejoice over the way God brings freedom and blessing to His children. The spirits are so insignificant!

How is it that our names come to be written in heaven? It is by His grace. If it is by grace, we have nothing to boast about. We should rejoice that we have been invited to participate in eternal life, the Kingdom of God.

God Opposes the Proud

There is one thing you should be afraid of, namely, your pride. First Peter 5:5 says, "All of you, clothe yourselves with humility toward one another, because, 'God opposes the proud but gives grace to the humble.'"

Sometimes we think the devil is at us and we need to take authority over him. But what is really happening is that God is after us and we need to repent and clothe ourselves with humility. Then we are better prepared to take authority over the devil.

One time, while praying for deliverance, a spirit spoke to me through the person, saying, "Do you think you are going to get away with this?" The promise of the Scriptures—"nothing will harm you"—came to my mind, and I felt laughter rise up in me. That was a gift of the Holy Spirit. If I were to laugh in my own strength, in some way thinking I was untouchable, I might be in for some trouble.

This lesson was reinforced to me very clearly after one of our conferences. Janet and I were walking away from the last talk. "That was amazing; it went so well," I said. No sooner had I gotten the words out of my mouth than I tripped and stubbed my toe. As soon as I stubbed that toe, I started to repent for my pride. It was an illustration. God loves us so much He will allow opposition to come to us so that we will not be proud.

I do a number of things to clothe myself in humility, preparing myself for deliverance prayer.

First, I repent of my sins. Before a seminar or an appointment, I confess my sins. Asking the help of the Holy Spirit, I search my conscience and confess the sins I am aware of. If we confess our sins, they are covered by the sacrifice of Jesus Christ. I know one minister who did not want to pray for deliverance because he was afraid his sins would be revealed. Satan can deter us through pride and a lack of confidence in the mercy of God.

Second, I offer myself to Him. I want to be His instrument. My constant prayer is, "Keep me out of Your way, Lord, and keep me from my pride."

Third, when I pray for others, *I remember it is the Lord doing the work.* I consciously try to follow His lead and not rely on my own understanding.

Fourth, I ask others to intercede for me in my continuing deliverance ministry. I have no idea what I have been protected from because of others' prayers. They pray for Janet and me and those to whom we are ministering. God answers the prayers of His saints who come to Him on behalf of others and for the sake of the Kingdom.

Fifth, I pray for protection. It is important to enter into the battle asking for God's protection. There are many wonderful prayers that people use to pray for protection from the enemy. Some pray these daily. These prayers are intended to be an expression of our dependence on God. Done in this way they can produce much fruit. But sometimes these spiritual warfare prayers are prayed as an expression of fear, repeated over and over. The person places more trust in saying the prayer than in the Lord and His promises.

If something should happen to me that appears to be retaliation from the devil, I do not blame the devil or God. I first look at my sin, especially the sin of pride, and repent. Then I rebuke the devil.

Testing Through Trials

We all grow through trials, through times of testing. You will experience internal death and struggle as God strips away the things that resist His love. If you serve Him in deliverance ministry or any ministry that advances the Kingdom of God, you will probably experience the struggle more intensely. Do not let yourself be distracted from the spiritual disciplines, the regular practice of your faith.

When you witness the incredible mercy of God displayed in people's lives, there is a wonderful consolation and sense of intimacy with Jesus. With that sense of His presence and the pressing needs of so many people, you may be tempted to move away from the basics: daily prayer, study, dying to yourself and making love your aim in all relationships. Jesus was in constant demand. The need was so very great. And yet He did not fail to find time for prayer. He had an intimacy with the Father.

Do you think that your church, ministry, prayer group or family is being hassled by the enemy? Do you sense that you are under great spiritual warfare? You may be, but sometimes we give the devil too much credit. Humble yourself before the Lord. (The enemy can do nothing to you that God does not permit for your ultimate benefit and the advancement of His Kingdom.) Then stand in faith against him, pray and intercede, asking God's protection, renounce your fears and stand in a place of confidence knowing that no weapon formed against you shall prosper (see Isaiah 54:17). Our response determines how long it will take for us to receive the victory Jesus has won for us.

The Devil's Weakness

Satan is a very intelligent being, much smarter than we are. If God were not on our side, we would be hopelessly overmatched. He has power, but the only way he can use it is through human beings (as God permits). If he is to strike back at God, he must do it through us and to us. The question is, If Satan is so smart, why does he keep doing things to advance the purposes of God? History is filled with examples of how satanic ploys to destroy God's servants have backfired. Can you imagine Satan's delight the day the fruit of all his labor was rewarded? The day human beings, called to be God's children, rejected God's very Son? All of Satan's fury was unleashed upon Jesus as He endured the agonizing death upon the cross. Finally the devil struck back at God, not simply by attacking God's children, but this time by directing a blow to God Himself. His greatest victory was his greatest defeat. In response to every attempt by Satan to destroy Him, Jesus did not sin: He surrendered to God. He forgave. No one took His life; He gave it freely. If the devil is so intelligent, why did he do it? Couldn't he see what was coming?

Or could it be he knew what would happen but did not care? A drug addict needs his fix. As the addiction increases, he no longer cares about the consequences. "So what if I may die; everyone is going to die." The harm he does to himself and others is insignificant. The thing that has become his master consumes him. He has lost his freedom and forsaken his dignity.

In a similar way Satan has lost his freedom. He has been mastered by his hatred. He has chosen the path of rebellion. He is a thief who comes only to kill and destroy (see John 10:10). He was a murderer from the beginning (see John 8:44). His "fix" is to destroy what God has made. He may be intelligent, but he is not free to use that intelligence wisely. A demon might boast about what he has done to a person, even though it may reveal the key to that person's liberation. Why? Because it is a demon's nature to do so. Demons have forsaken the names that God gave them as angels. And with that their God-given identities have been lost for eternity. Now their identities are found not in who they are as much as in what they do. They are simply a spirit of greed, a spirit of hatred and so forth.

You may see this dynamic in someone you know. Someone who has become completely self-focused has lost the value of relationships. The fact that he or she is a son or daughter, a father or mother, a husband or wife, has become lost. The way such people understand themselves is by what they do. It is simply a matter of time until the revelation of their emptiness crushes them. This is Satan's ultimate doom, to be banished from the earth, lost in a purposeless eternity.

But for now Satan seeks to be worshiped. He seeks to take the place of God in our lives. This is who he is, and this is what his servants look like.

Chained Dog

Augustine taught that Satan is like a chained dog barking madly. Imagine yourself walking down a path, darkened by overhanging trees. Suddenly a ferocious dog jumps at you, barking. You see its teeth and not much else. Fear overtakes you, and if you are not frozen you run. Many believers have a fear of the devil. They listen to the growl but fail to see the chain around the neck. Smith Wigglesworth understood the chain and knew it could not be broken.

The apostle Paul tells us that the devil has been disarmed; he is powerless. In the same way that captured soldiers were marched through the streets in humiliation, so, too, have the devil and his troops been humiliated by the triumph of the cross (see Colossians 2:14–15).

The devil's influence came through the fall of man and continues through our sinful rebellion against God. The Law, which tells us we have sinned, is the basis by which the devil accuses us. Jesus conquered Satan and invites us into a radically new world. In this new Kingdom, our sins are forgiven. The power of the Law to condemn us has been broken. At one time we based our sense of value and acceptance on how perfectly we kept the rules. At the cross we find a new way of living based on the mercy of God and on our identification with the sinless One, the One who perfectly fulfilled the Law. It is not an identification that rests simply in our willpower or our thinking. We are given His very life in the Holy Spirit, who empowers us to live as Jesus did. We no longer look to justify ourselves and to argue our case for admittance to heaven based on how good we have been. Instead we trust in what Jesus has done for us. He has justified us, and it is His garment of righteousness we seek to put on daily.

Satan has been defeated; he has been disarmed. We do not need to fear his bark. But there remains a need for caution. Satan is bound by a chain, which means we can foolishly walk into his territory and come under his influence. It also means we can forget the basis of our freedom, forsaking the new way of living in Jesus for a life of self-justification, no longer seeing the chain but only the dog's teeth.

The best preparation for the ministry of deliverance is to live it. Intercession, repentance, forgiveness, renunciation, rebuking and receiving the blessing. You will be tested, and you need to respond. If you take up the work of praying for others, you will hear the bark of the enemy. You will need to learn to look at the chain and know that the enemy has been bound.

Freedom Is Found in the Truth

When the devil tempted Jesus in the desert, Jesus relied on the truth of the Scriptures to defeat the enemy's lies. Later He spoke to us all: "If you hold to my teaching, you are really my disciples. Then *you will know the truth,* and the truth will set you free" (John 8:31–32, emphasis added).

Fear of the devil is based on deception, not on the truth. The truth is found in the following Scripture verses:

Satan has been disarmed

He forgave us all our sins, having canceled the written code, with its regulations, that was against us and that stood opposed to us; he took it away, nailing it to the cross. And having *disarmed the powers and authorities,* he made a public spectacle of them, triumphing over them by the cross.

Colossians 2:14–15, emphasis added

Nothing will harm us if we walk in Jesus' authority

"I have given you authority to trample on snakes and scorpions and to overcome all the power of the enemy; nothing will harm you."

Luke 10:19

Nothing can separate us from the love of God

For I am convinced that neither death nor life, neither angels nor demons, neither the present nor the future, nor any powers, neither height nor depth, nor anything else in all creation, will be able to separate us from the love of God that is in Christ Jesus our Lord.

Romans 8:38–39

You will not be overcome by the temptation of the devil

No temptation has seized you except what is common to man. And God is faithful; He will not let you be tempted beyond what you can bear. But when you are tempted, he will also provide a way out so that you can stand up under it.

1 Corinthians 10:13

All things work together for our benefit

And we know that in all things God works for the good of those who love him, who have been called according to his purpose.

Romans 8:28

If we embrace these truths and understand the nature of the devil's threats and his limitations, we, like Smith Wigglesworth, will no longer have to trust in what our eyes see. Rather we can say to the devil, "Oh, it is only you!"

Let the name of the Lord be praised, both now and forevermore. From the rising of the sun to the place where it sets, the name of the LORD is to be praised. The LORD is exalted over all the nations, his glory above the heavens.

Psalm 113:2–4

Lord, fill my heart with praise. Let Your praise be on my lips and the joy of salvation be in my heart. Let me declare with the Scriptures, "The LORD is my light and my salvation—whom shall I fear? The LORD is the stronghold of my life—of whom shall I be afraid?" (Psalm 27:1).

If we are not deterred by fear, the enemy will surely try to take advantage of our ignorance and mistakes. In the next chapter I want to share with you some mistakes you can avoid.

12

How Not to Pray for Deliverance

> Oh, good gentle Jesus! Let popes, pastors, and everyone
> else blush for shame at our foolishness and pride and self-
> indulgence, when we see such generosity, goodness, and
> boundless love on our creator's part!
>
> Catherine of Siena

Seven years ago, on our first trip to Slovakia, we taught on
evangelization and the Christian life. During one of the sessions, a young woman began to manifest the presence of an
evil spirit. After the session we assisted the priest who prayed
for her. We had some experience—more than the priest—but
we were unable to help her and left the country knowing she
had not been delivered. My heart ached for her. A seed was
planted that day—a hunger to learn more, to better help
those in need and to teach others what I had been given. I
was not yet ready, but I believed this was a divine encounter,
a preparation for the future, and someday I would return to
Slovakia.

At the time of our second trip, that seed had grown and
yielded an abundance of fruit. This time we spent two and

a half days with a group of forty people who led missions in Slovakia and beyond. We taught them about deliverance, prayed with them, taught them how to pray for others and formed ministry teams. Their training continued over the larger weekend conference, attended by a hundred additional people. Prior to lunch on Saturday the teams began to pray for those who requested prayer. Before the afternoon session, Janet and I met briefly with the teams. They were still a bit timid. I reminded them there is only one measure of success: that the person leaves knowing he has been loved and encouraged to continue trusting the Lord. "The first time I used this method to pray for deliverance I did not do so well," I told them. "But I did not do any harm either. Everyone you pray for is sent by the Lord and is part of your training. Remember the lessons you learn from each person. Stand by one another, encourage one another and pray for one another. My wife, Janet, stood by me; it was her prayer and encouragement that kept me going."

By the end of the day there was great rejoicing, as many were set free. The team learned how to help others cooperate with Jesus as He set them free. I announced that anyone who received prayer but did not feel he had gotten help should come forward. The three who responded to that invitation were quickly set free.

One said she had forgiven two people, but she still felt a gripping sensation in her throat. The team had led her in forgiveness, but because of their inexperience they did not realize a spirit of unforgiveness needed to be renounced. I led her to do so, and she was set free.

Another woman had begun to weep at the morning session. Desperate, she said, "I do not know what it is. I have forgiven everyone I know." A thought came to my mind.

"Have you ever been in love?" I asked.

"Yes." She thought she had dealt with the rejection, but she had not. It had been buried. She left very happy.

175

All three were set free because the inexperienced team had done its job. They had listened, showed compassion, prayed and helped each individual respond to Jesus.

My Journey

I tell you this story to encourage you, but now I want to back up and tell you about some of the mistakes I've made seeking to help people find freedom. I learn more from my mistakes than I do any other way.

Remember, Satan is a master of deception and confusion. I know people who at one time prayed with others for deliverance with some success. Later, because of mistakes, inexperience and confusion, they stopped praying for deliverance. This happened to me. After several forays into deliverance prayer over the course of 25 years, I pulled back from time to time determining I would pray for the healing of others but stay away from deliverance (unless God was very clear about it). Was it not yet God's time? Was it due to the confusion the devil brings to the deliverance ministry? Was it my immaturity? I needed a teacher. God sent me a teacher in 1996.

That year Christians from diverse backgrounds in the Greater Philadelphia area responded to a call to gather for 31 consecutive nights at a large church pastored by Dr. Benjamin Smith. The guest speaker was Randy Clark, a pastor known for his part in bringing renewal, healing and teaching.

In preparation for the meetings, a team from Argentina came to teach on deliverance ministry. They believed that a successful evangelistic crusade needed to introduce people to the saving power of Jesus, but also to Jesus the deliverer. If people come to Jesus and remain in bondage, they may quickly be robbed of the full power of their encounter with the Lord.

That is where I met Pablo Bottari. Pablo was a barber in 1984 when he met Carlos Annacondia, a businessman who led large crusades in Argentina. Pablo later went into full-time ministry training and oversaw the deliverance tents for Annacondia. At that time he estimated he had prayed with or overseen fifty thousand people who had received deliverance ministry.

Pablo did three important things for me. First, he prayed for me. As he spoke words of blessing over me, I once again embraced the gifts God had given me, the gifts of understanding and compassion. Second, Pablo taught his ten-step method.[1] His teaching was characterized by love and compassion. He taught me how to pray for people so that, if they did not get free right away, they would still feel loved. He taught me how to minimize the physical manifestations of evil that people are often subjected to in deliverance. Third, he took me alongside him and let me watch, and then he sent me out to pray using his model for deliverance.

Since then I have prayed for hundreds of people and taught hundreds of others how to pray for deliverance in four different countries. New freedom to pray for others came by understanding how to avoid the mistakes I had made and the mistakes or abuses I had seen in other deliverance ministries. In the past God used me as an instrument to set the captives free. Then, because it got a bit messy, I'd stopped praying for others to be liberated. I know many people who went though a similar pattern. The devil can use our ignorance and stupidity to keep us from fruitfulness. But the Lord is a good and faithful teacher. He uses our mistakes to teach us.

Mistakes to Avoid

Before I share what I have learned about how to pray for deliverance, I would like to list some of the mistakes I have made or observed others make. Such mistakes serve to discredit deliverance ministry and rightfully contribute to the caution pastors and church leaders exhibit toward this ministry.

As you read the following list of mistakes that can and should be avoided, consider these overriding guidelines:

1. If your heart is right, you can have confidence that God will cover your mistakes as you learn.
2. Never place God in a box or get in His way. Sometimes God chooses to deliver a person with little participation on your part.

Mistake 1: Recklessly Invading a Soul

Back in those early days of discovery, I received a panic call from someone in our prayer group. "Could you come over? We have a problem. This older woman we were visiting is manifesting, and we cannot get the demon to leave." They were frightened because the woman was blacking out and speaking with another voice, which did not respond to their commands. With great dread I went over. Those praying with the woman had read a book about casting out demons. When the woman was willing to receive prayer, they commanded the demons to leave. They got more than they bargained for. Fortunately, I was able to bring the woman to peace and end the session on a relatively peaceful note.

I learned an important lesson that day. Never go where you are not invited. A person must take responsibility for his life. A person who is not ready to identify and renounce the demons may not be ready to live without them. If a person has lived with bitterness since childhood and has not accepted the Gospel, it is not appropriate to command bitterness to go. Such was the case with this elderly woman. You will only cause a power encounter, and the struggle for the soul may manifest. Even if the evil spirit should leave, it will come right back, perhaps making the situation worse. Share the Good News, and get the person hooked up with the Lord first.

Mistake 2: Focusing on the Demon and Not the Person

Always focus on the person who needs help, not the demon. The compassion of Jesus should lead the way. Testimonies of deliverance ought to produce hope, not fear.

Some models for deliverance not only expect manifestations of evil, they rely on them. This model got national television exposure when NBC's *Dateline* aired a deliverance session. The day before the planned event, *Dateline* asked the pastor leading the session what he expected to happen the next day. "I expect that an evil presence, which has been tormenting this man for a long, long time, is going to manifest. And it's going to start talking back to us, and it's going to physically express itself in his body. And there's going to be a break point at which, with a great deal of protestations, it is going to leave. And then, you're going to see a peace settle on this man, which is nothing short of miraculous."

It is not surprising that this is exactly what happened. (Unfortunately it took five hours that day and six additional sessions for the man to finally declare that he was free.) This model focuses on the confrontation with demons and emphasizes commanding the spirit to reveal itself, tormenting it with Scripture (or religious objects). Though the model I present in chapter 14 is very different, I was pleased to see how faithful, loving and humble this minister was as he sought to help the man. The before-and-after pictures did demonstrate a wonderful change in the man's countenance.

Mistake 3: Casting Out the Demon but Not Discovering and Sealing Off the Entryway

My focus is the person and helping him or her deal with foundational issues that serve as entryways for evil spirits. But I have not always had this insight. In 1973, Janet and I were close to a young man who had a number of internal conflicts, especially related to his father. These conflicts surfaced in his work relationships. Don asked for deliverance prayer. We had never prayed with anyone for deliverance before. We decided to spend the day in prayer and fasting and then pray at dinnertime. The prayer did not take long: We rebuked the devil, and Don's face twisted and took on the appearance of evil. Janet said, "It is hatred."

I had never seen such hatred as what manifested on his face. What was hidden deep in his soul was exposed, and it hated us for exposing it. "In the name of Jesus, I command hatred to leave," I spoke out loud. Immediately it left, and Don's face returned to normal. At that moment we heard a yell and what sounded like a dresser being thrown down the steps from behind the adjoining wall of our neighbor's house. The disturbance shook us, causing us fear. Being inexperienced, we were easily intimidated and deceived. We did not consider that other issues might need prayer. We never led Don in a prayer to forgive his father. We merely gave the Lord thanks and ordered pizza.

We did not go far enough with Don. We dealt with a spirit but not the root, its entryway. To seal an entryway means to lead the person through repentance for specific sins, forgiveness of specific individuals, renunciation of lies and the spirits behind the lies, and then complete the process by a prayer of blessing for the person.

I admit that after that night we did not want anything more to do with deliverance ministry. It was only after a year, motivated by concern and compassion, that I prayed again this way for Sheila.

Mistake 4: Failing to Give Follow-up Instructions

The next year, in 1974, I counseled Sheila, a woman who had said (among other things), "Every day on the way home from work, I feel this compulsion to turn my car and drive off the side of the bridge." I had read a few books on deliverance ministry but had little experience dealing with evil spirits. This sure sounded like the work of the devil. Wanting to help, I commanded every evil spirit to leave her in the name of Jesus. Immediately her face disfigured and her eyes became piercing. She looked up at me and demanded, "Do you know what you are doing?"

"Yes, Jesus loves you and He has come to set you free." My response reflected what I believed, but my thoughts were very different. I felt like a grammar school kid caught roaming the halls when a stern voice demanded, "Are you supposed to be here?"

My inner response was, *No, I don't know what I am doing,* and I wondered if I was supposed to be here in a battle with the enemy. I knew one thing: The only other person I felt I could take her to was a six-hour drive away. I knew a second thing: I could rely on the Lord. This was His work and I had to trust Him. I got another person to join me and enlisted others to intercede for her deliverance outside. We prayed and we commanded, but nothing seemed to change. The evil presence was still there, and Sheila was under stress. We could not leave her in this state. Ultimately we had three two-hour sessions. Finally the Lord revealed the identity of the evil spirit, and when we named the area of bondage and commanded it to go, it left. What relief and joy we all felt! Looking back I think of how merciful God was to all of us. Yet how unfortunate it was that Sheila had to go through hours of unnecessary struggle.

When we prayed for Sheila, as with Don, we did not know how to interview the person or how to look for the root cause. We sent Sheila on her way knowing the name of one of her enemies but not the root cause for its presence in her. As a result we did not give her adequate guidance in how to remain free. We did not help her to understand Satan's plans or areas where she was weak.

Mistake 5: Failing to Bring Filling and Blessing

When a person has been set free, the process is completed by filling the void with the love of God and a blessing of the person's identity. Even in the beginning we understood that we should pray for a filling of the Holy Spirit, that the house should not be left empty (see Luke 11:24–26). What we did not know is that this very important prayer may require more than a general prayer for the love and light of the Holy Spirit to fill the void. Often it is the absence of blessing—the affirmation of one's identity and destiny—that leaves a person open to bondage by evil spirits. Therefore, filling the void may require inspired words of affirmation, acceptance and confidence that he will fulfill God's special plan for his life. The love of God needs to be released into the area that has been bound. It is not enough to drive away fear; one must experience God's love. It is not enough to break the power of rejection; one needs to know his acceptance in Christ.

Mistake 6: Failing to Interview Properly

Another year passed. Henry, a friend of mine, came to me and said he believed he needed deliverance. A mature Christian leader, he had a wonderful gift of teaching. He understood as much about deliverance as I did, so we began to pray. In response to the command in the name of Jesus, an immediate manifestation of evil took place; it appeared that the bones in his skull were shifting to create a tortured expression.

One session led to another, and then another. He so wanted to be free. We began to pray weekly for him. I sought advice wherever I could. We took him to a minister in another city who had a deliverance ministry. Bizarre manifestations of fear and torment punctuated the session. Something seemed to lift, but the deliverance was not complete. We were encouraged to continue praying weekly. Then we heard of a man several hours away who had a deliverance ministry. He invited us to come to one of his healing services and said he would pray for my friend. No change, but only confusion, resulted from this meeting. I went with Henry to a Christian counselor who prayed for deliverance. It promised to be a long and expensive process, and we had no reason to believe it would end any differently. Eventually we agreed to stop meeting until we received more wisdom from the Lord.

Back then we did not understand some of the things I now consider basics, such as an extensive interview (which I will describe in chapter 13) and breaking the enemy's power through renunciation and forgiveness. It was clear we did not understand what we needed to know. And nobody we consulted told us to stop or move in another direction. Nevertheless, I now believe the severity of the manifestations was unnecessary. If we knew about interviewing and renouncing prior to casting out a demon, we would have avoided so much unnecessary discomfort for my friend. I thank God that Henry initiated these meetings and that he was mature and stable enough to handle the trauma he went through. I also praise God that He is my teacher and that often our best lessons come through our failures.

As I said above, at this point healing prayer was looking a lot better to me than deliverance prayer. As I focused my prayer for others on healing, demons stopped manifesting and God stopped sending me people with obvious need for deliverance. That was fine with me. I was very dissatisfied with the long-term results and the process involved in deliverance. I was thinking, "Let somebody else do it. Please!"

Mistake 7: Being Fascinated with the Manifestations and What the Demons Say

The only thing worth noting that a demon says is something that reveals his entryway, his identity or his plan of destruction. I read in the paper that the pope stopped to pray for a girl manifesting an evil spirit. The priest who later prayed for the girl said, "How happy the demon was. He had some laughs. He even had the girl say to me, 'Not even your boss (that is, the pope) has been able to do anything with me!'"

What a shame. The father of lies (John 8:44) gets enough space in the newspaper. Do we have to give him more?

Mistake 8: Focusing on the Confrontation and Not on the Person

At the beginning of one of my seminars a man said he was looking forward to kicking out some demons. He sounded like a teenager out on a Friday night cruising for trouble. At the end of the seminar this man came up to me, humbly saying, "I have a lot to learn." Some of the books I have read about deliverance speak a lot about the devil and his works. They give vivid details about the deliverance session but little about the person. We need to focus on the person we hope will be delivered.

On some of our trips we spend over six hours a day (in addition to teaching) praying with people for deliverance. While it is a joy to see people set free, if the focus of our prayer was confronting demons, we would be totally drained after one session.

Mistake 9: Praying from a Place of Pride or Fear

These are such dangerous mistakes that I addressed them in chapter 11.

Mistake 10: Praying for Deliverance for Someone Who Never Repented or Trusted in Jesus

One young man who came to me had obvious need for deliverance from evil spirits; he had some significant psychological problems as well. A highly respected pastor sent him to me, and so I agreed to meet with him. I listened carefully to the bizarre lifestyle of confused relationships. He carried with him prayer books and several holy objects, including a "relic of the true cross." He wanted me to pray for him. He went to church and identified with it. I shared with him the basic message of the Gospel and sought to lead him in a prayer of surrender. He did not seem to realize the importance of surrendering to Jesus. We did not connect. It could be that he needed deliverance in order to surrender, but I believe he had neither heard nor fully responded to the call to repent and surrender to the Savior. It would have been a big mistake for me to begin praying for deliverance. He needed much more than I could offer him. I prayed for healing and blessing. I prayed for a greater openness to the Savior. If the person does not sincerely want to submit to Jesus, deliverance prayer will not help him.

Mistake 11: Praying for Deliverance for Those Who Do Not Want to Be Free

I have spoken to people who seem to draw their identity from the abuse they went through or even the process of healing and deliverance they are currently experiencing. Taking the next step to freedom requires great courage. The desire for human affirmation may be greater than their desire to be free. Someone who has not been affirmed in their identity may need a lot of time in the community of believers to leave the old and embrace their new identity in Christ. Applying the principles in this book in the context of "helping a friend" is extremely valuable for a person like this. If it becomes obvious that they are merely seeking attention and do not really want to be free, you should not lead them through deliverance. Pray for them, bless them and counsel them. A person may not be ready to take responsibility for their life prior to deliverance, but you should be able to discern the desire to be free and the desire to take responsibility to walk in that freedom.

Another man who was deeply disoriented and affected by the occult came to a church service regularly. The congregation welcomed him but made sure he sat in the back. Two large men were assigned to sit with him. At just about every service he would run to the altar in a rage, seemingly to attack the pastor. I was told he had been delivered several times but became demonized again. One night when I was there, he was wrestled to the ground (to prevent his attack) and a number of church leaders gathered around commanding the spirits to leave. Nothing seemed to change. I'm not sure if he liked the attention, but I am sure he did not want to be free. He was not ready.

Mistake 12: Having the Person Rely on the Minister Instead of on Jesus

Often at conferences long lines form for the conference leader to pray for healing or deliverance. While God does use some people more often than others, no one is able to do anything that God has not already planted in his heart. If God is the initiator, then ordinary believers can pray for healing and deliverance and see results.

Many times those who have been set free think the person who helped them is the only one who can help in the future. Everything I do when I pray for people is meant to teach basic principles about freedom in Christ. These principles help the person realize who he is and the authority he has in Jesus. Combined with supportive relationships in the body of Christ, these principles will help him to continue to rely on Jesus, his deliverer.

Mistake 13: Judging Success or Failure Merely on the Driving Out of the Demon

The true test of success is whether the person experienced being loved. The person also should leave your presence encouraged and trusting in the Lord.

The following is an example of looking for demons and failing to love the person. A woman wrote me a letter, explaining her experience. It demonstrates how very badly someone can be wounded by sincere, misinformed Christians trying to drive out demons.

"I was invited by a friend to someone's house where they were having a small prayer gathering. I thought I was just going there for the fellowship. Anyway, when they wanted to pray for me, I said okay. However, some unusual manifestations began to occur. What happened after that was of more concern to me and left me frightened and very upset. The six women who were there were trying to deliver me of several demonic forces (lying spirits, incest, death spirit, etc.), without success, as they supposed. They yelled at me, threw me around and poured oil in my mouth to drink, and told me I spoke in 'false tongues' and needed deliverance from 'familiar spirits' from past generations.

"With the small amount of teaching and practice that I have had in deliverance ministry, I know that this is not the way to minister to someone. However, I respected their ministry, and believed what they were telling me and allowed them to do this. It left me quite confused, frightened and tormented."

This is a clear example of looking for demons and failing to love the person. Even if demons had left I would judge this as unsuccessful.

If you have prayed with someone for deliverance and no release is evident, know that you have helped that person if he leaves feeling the love of God and knowing better how to take responsibility for his life. You and I do not deliver anyone. Jesus does. Do not allow yourself to be placed in a situation where anyone, even yourself, expects that you will deliver someone from an evil spirit. This expectation will generate pressure on you. The results may be that we try too hard and fail to know when it is right to stop.

A preacher once said that God is able to take manure and make fertilizer out of it. As you continue on your journey, don't judge yourself too harshly, for all things are worked to the good of those who love God (see Romans 8:28). He is faithful. He demonstrates His faithfulness in us. Paul rejoiced over the Philippians as he considered God's faithfulness, "being confident of this, that he who began a good work in you will carry it on to completion until the day of Christ Jesus" (Philippians 1:6).

Above all, love each other deeply, because love covers over a multitude of sins.

1 Peter 4:8

Lord, I am fully capable of making many of the mistakes mentioned in this chapter. As I walk in humility, depending on Your grace, I am confident that Your love will cover my many mistakes and sins. Let me boldly follow Your example and wash the feet of those You send me.

Make love your aim, and earnestly desire the spiritual gifts.

1 Corinthians 14:1, RSV

It is not enough to know what mistakes to avoid. Now let's look at how to help someone receive his deliverance.

13

Walking Someone
through Deliverance

"Don't you believe that I am in the Father, and that the Father
is in me? The words I say to you are not just my own. Rather,
it is the Father, living in me, who is doing his work."

John 14:10

Jesus Is Our Teacher

Jesus is our teacher. He has shown us the way. Just as the Father was living in Him, doing His work, so we have the privilege of Jesus living in us, doing *His* work. Deliverance is *His* work. Our goal is to allow God to do His work through us.

Some people are intimidated by talk of deliverance from evil spirits. I prefer to use the term "freedom from the influence of evil spirits" because it does not imply a single big event; it is really a matter of degrees. We all need ongoing freedom from the influence of evil spirits. We face temptations and oppression daily. We are freed from their influence

189

by the grace of God released through all sorts of spiritual activities, such as prayer, Bible reading, confession of sin, worship, sacraments, as well as through renunciation and the word of command. Having said that, in this chapter, I focus on the specific prayer session in which an evil spirit's power in a person's life can be broken.

When we pray for people we should create an atmosphere of love and acceptance, where renouncing the works of the devil seems more a normal expression of repentance than an abnormal one. Many times people who are touched by God during a deliverance session remember every detail of what happened. To me this shows that it is a unique teaching opportunity that brings with it a responsibility. We must remember that we are teachers as well as instruments of His grace.

Clear Objectives

As I have said before, our objective is to love someone with the love of Jesus and to *assist* him in getting free from the influence of evil spirits.

In seeking deliverance, some may want what God does not wish to give. No matter how much freedom any of us receives, we will always have seasons of suffering; there will always be "crosses to bear" with Christ. Our faith is purified through testing. With every test we pass, we are building a history (Israel marked the events of their history with piles of stones). It is a history of God's faithfulness so that during our next trial (in which we will be tested but never more than we can bear) we will remember His faithfulness and trust Him.

Someone who seeks deliverance as part of a lifelong attempt to escape pain will ultimately be disappointed. We need to understand the place and role of suffering if we are to help that person cooperate with what Jesus is doing in his life.

190

Suffering is usually not the issue; it is one's response to suffering that brings either freedom or bondage. We may always have the cross in our lives, but we do not have to live without joy or hope. God is at work in the suffering of a believer to liberate him from bondage and bring him into His purpose for his life. In deliverance we are unlocking doors that have shut us off from receiving God's love. We can know freedom from the heaviness, the compulsions and the fears that keep us in bondage and keep us from loving God and others. This is not the same as being free from suffering.

If someone is manifesting the presence of an evil spirit, he should be helped to gain control of himself—as I will discuss in chapter 14. I have chosen to walk through basics here and then discuss manifestations later.

The Team

Generally it is important to have two or three people pray as a team, with one person leading the session and prayer.[1] This leader should be the principal one to address the person seeking help. The one or two other team members intercede, seek discernment and give support, even as they are being trained to be leaders themselves. Anyone present to support in intercession should not break the connection between the person leading and the one being prayed for. Someone having discernment should wait for an appropriate time to communicate with the leader. Only the leader should place hands on the person while praying for deliverance, though all may join in the time of blessing.

Demons respond to the authority of Jesus being manifest through a person. The leader needs to take up the authority God has given him. If it is not clear who on the team has the authority (and responsibility) for the session, the demon will be less responsive to your commands. Also, the person you are praying for will feel less secure and perhaps be less vulnerable to you and less responsive to the Holy Spirit. The authority of Jesus will not be manifested if the team is confused or not in unity. The team must be united and supportive of the leader.

If a man is leading and praying for a woman, it is extremely important that a woman be present for support; the same is true if a woman is praying for a man. This will reassure the person as well as help protect from demons that may manifest in a sexual way. When praying for a woman, I especially appreciate Janet's presence. As a woman she is more sensitive to certain issues. She is also very quick to point out when someone may be relating to me in an inappropriate way.

Getting Started

Before asking any questions of someone who has come for deliverance prayer, I do everything I can to help him feel relaxed, welcomed, accepted and loved. (In this chapter, for illustrative purposes, let's assume the person I'm praying for is male.) I want the person to know that I am thrilled he has come, that he is worth my time and that he is safe. Humor and a smile can go a long way in relieving anxiety.

Usually I begin with a verbal prayer, but not always. It depends on the person and my own frame of mind. If I am distracted and not aware of God's design for setting him free, I may ask the Holy Spirit to lead the person's sharing through our interview and to help me understand what Jesus wants to do. Other times I pray because the person expects it or I believe it will help him relax and get in touch with his heart. Whether I stop to pray or not, I am in constant prayer, "Come, Holy Spirit." *Prayer is the overall context for the ministry of deliverance.* I remind myself that if this person is to be set free, it is because Jesus is doing it; I am just an instrument. (I am often amazed at how the Holy Spirit directs the interview.) I am there primarily to help the person find liberation from demonic influence; any counseling that goes on is secondary. The prayers and commands that will bear fruit are those that agree with God's agenda for the person's life. I am listening for what the Lord may reveal.

Core Interview

"What would you like Jesus to do for you?" This is a question I typically ask at the beginning of the interview. It helps prepare us for targeted prayer. Other times I ask, "Tell me what is going on."

I usually listen at length. Sometimes it takes a while for people to say what they really want to say. I am listening and waiting: listening for hatred, resentment, envy, pride, vengeance, rage, bitterness, unforgiveness, fear, traumas, fixations, complexes, doubts, insecurity, phobias. I jot down anything that may need to be renounced or the names of any who may need to be forgiven. I am seeking any insight or revelation the Lord may give me.

After I get a picture of what is going on, I usually ask the person to tell me about his parents. As I listen I am looking to connect the dots between any pattern of difficulty arising from the relationship with his parents in the early years and what is being experienced now.

Find out if the person is going to church, receiving counseling and being supported by a network of godly friends. These things can be as (or more) important to the person as deliverance. All this information will aid in discerning how to proceed.

Do not allow yourself to feel pressured to help someone you feel is not a good candidate. This is a bit subjective, but, for instance, if there is reason to be suspicious of deeper psychological or psychiatric problems, such as schizophrenia or paranoid psychosis, you might ask these questions: Has anyone ever labeled this as something else? Have you ever been hospitalized or medicated? Are you on medication now, and are you taking the medication regularly?

I would not recommend a full deliverance session for someone in a psychological or emotional crisis. It is much better if someone is stabilized so that he can participate in the process and not misunderstand how you are trying to help him. If he is under professional care, I recommend a consultation with the therapist. You may not feel comfortable dealing with the person's issues or with the way the person relates to you. He may be too controlling or manipulative for you. One man I know who has prayed for many people often stops short of praying for those who have a similar sexual history as he does. If you are just beginning to pray for others, try to be reasonably confident that the Lord sent this person to you and you're not taking on more than you are prepared for.

The word *interview* may imply that I'm asking a series of set questions.[2] Although I ask many questions, the emphasis is always on listening and trusting the Holy Spirit to reveal what is important. Many times I sense that the Holy Spirit prompts the question. Recently I asked a man if the Lord said anything to him when he was baptized in the Holy Spirit. Emotion surfaced for the first time in the interview. "I will never abandon you," he said. The Lord had previously spoken to his deepest need. My asking an unscripted question had allowed him to name *the* issue in his life. He was delivered of bondage after renouncing abandonment and a few related spirits.

Throughout the interview I take notes and listen for insight in four areas.

1. Why has he come?

Is he ready to surrender to the Lord? Is he desperate? Is it God moving him or simply his pain, or both? Some may ask for prayer wanting attention or comfort, but they don't really want to be free. Some have repented, forgiven and exposed the darkness, and all they need is the prayer of authority and blessing and encouragement. If this does not become obvious I may ask, "Do you want to be free?" People need to say what they want. This helps clarify their true desires. It also helps them remember that asking is an important part of the process by which the Lord sets them free. Jesus asked the blind man what he wanted, even though it was clear the man was blind (see Mark 10:51).

2. Are there spiritual obstacles?

Any involvement in the occult will be an obstacle and must be dealt with. It may also be the root. A trip to the fortuneteller or palm reader, tarot cards, séances, Ouija boards, horoscopes, psychic hot lines, witchcraft, divination, black magic, voodoo—any of these, even if done in "fun," should be renounced. Spirits that come to a person through these means can be like a cloud over his whole life, or they may keep him from processing life's experiences and moving into maturity. I am also listening for curses—negative words spoken by others that have taken on a life in the person's psyche. For example, one woman told me that she asked her mother if she was conceived as a mistake. Her mother's response: "You were not the mistake, you were the accident!" I am listening for self-inflicted curses such as "I hate myself."

Involvement in the occult seems to seal the spirits that are at work in someone's life; it seals Satan's plan, because an invitation was made. For example, you may have a problem with a sense of unworthiness that goes back to childhood. If you later go to a fortuneteller and are afflicted by the occult spirit working though her, the process to get free from the unworthiness becomes complicated. The occult spirit is guarding the door. It has to be told it is no longer welcome and must go. Many spirits leave as we pursue the Lord, but these spirits must be told to leave. They have been invited, it is their place of rest and the invitation has given them a legal right. They will hold other spirits in their place. It is like the first room in a series of rooms. The occult spirit will obscure the door to the next room, keeping you from going deeper in the truth.[3]

3. Does he know Jesus?

When I interview someone I do not know I often say, "Tell me about your relationship with the Lord. Do you know Him in a personal way? When you think of God whom do you picture? Have you ever been 'saved' or had a conversion experience?" Those who know the Lord love to talk about Him and what He has done for them. The story of meeting Him is the most precious story they have to tell. Ask whatever question seems right for the person. Listen for what may be missing: relationship with the Father, Jesus or the Holy Spirit. Share with him about the Lord if he has never encountered the Savior. If he says the right words but something seems to be missing, prepare to lead the person in a recommitment to the Lord at the beginning of the session.

I prayed for a good man who dedicated his life to Christian service. During one seminar I taught, I shared an impression I had that someone was on the outside looking in, wondering if he really had a place in the Father's house. He came to me for deliverance. First I led him in a prayer recommitting his life to Jesus. Then I spent some time leading him to renounce and forgive. Something was missing. As time went on I realized the issue was surrendering to the Lord. Perhaps because of the issues we had addressed or perhaps because of the repetition, this time as I led him in prayer he surrendered to Jesus. He met the Savior. There is no greater deliverance than this.

4. Is there a need for repentance?

Finally, I am listening for significant sins, especially compulsive sins and unrepented sins. However, most people ask for deliverance because they *have* repented and still are not free. Sometimes "sin rationalization" has taken place, and not true repentance. For example, a woman who has had an abortion may not have taken full responsibility for her sin; the pressures on her at the time and the influence of the world may have minimized her sense of responsibility. I am also looking for sexual sins that have penetrated the soul. Sexual intimacy outside of marriage leaves a binding between people through which evil spirits may operate.

As I listen I try to discern the pattern. What is Satan's plan for this person's life? What is his plan to destroy this person? What is the root experience around which a destructive system of thinking has developed?

Finishing the Interview

I summarize verbally what I think the person has told me and share any insights I sense intuitively or learn from the Holy Spirit. Next I explain how I would like to proceed. I continue when I have received the person's permission to do so.

How quickly this all happens depends on how open someone's heart is to the Lord. The initial interview generally takes forty minutes or less, but we should never limit God to what we expect as the norm. During certain times and life seasons we are more open to the work of the Lord. At a conference retreat or after a church service, participants may be more sensitive to the work of the Holy Spirit in them. It may happen quickly if the Kingdom of God has exposed the darkness (resulting in a manifestation) or if the gift of discernment helps zero in on what God wants to do. One young woman was scheduled to leave our conference two days early, before we had a chance to pray for her. She asked Janet for a brief prayer and began to weep. Janet called me over to speak with her, and it seemed as if I knew her. Everything I asked, every prayer I prayed, generated a response.

In a matter of five minutes we had led her to renounce and forgive. She experienced what she describes as a great inner washing and a lifting of years of rejection. She stayed for the beginning of the next session to share her testimony of freedom and joy. She received what normally would have taken place after a long interview. Why? Simply because God loves His children, and He can use whomever He wants and do whatever He chooses.

The interview may be much simpler if you know the person or if God has given him a revelation of what he needs. For example, I prayed briefly with a woman on Friday night of a seminar. She came because she was oppressed. On the way home God brought to her mind something she heard when she was very young (too young to remember without God's help): that her mother had been unable to have children until she went to a fortuneteller. She renounced the demonic claim on her life and was set free.

Sometimes during the interview I am lost: "Help, Lord!" Sometimes I understand before someone has finished telling his story: "Praise God!" Normally I simply have a sense of how to start the prayer as I am praying, "Come, Lord Jesus. Show me the way."

The Deliverance Process

When you think you know a starting point, explain how you are going to proceed. For instance, I might say: "I am going to lead you in a prayer; first a prayer to Jesus asking Him to set you free, then declarations of forgiveness and renunciation. Is that okay? I will lead you based on what you told me and any discernment I receive. All you need to do is repeat after me. If I say something that is not true, please tell me. Don't pray what isn't true for you. Or, if you can say it better in your own words, please do so. After I start the prayer in a particular direction you can continue it, as you feel led."

It is important that the person pray for himself. I generally have the person repeat after me. (I lead the prayer this way for the sake of time, and it works well with gifts I have been given.) Other times I will just suggest the topic and ask the person to speak to Jesus about his pain and his decision to forgive. Listening to the person's prayer and expressions of forgiveness often reveals areas of bondage. I then have him repeat after me the declarations of renunciation.

It is important to be relaxed and comfortable. You don't want to communicate any tension or anxiety. Don't try to make something happen. I usually ask if it is okay to hold the person's hand or touch an arm or shoulder. Touching connects you with the person. It helps to keep your focus on the person, not the demons.[4]

If the person does not know Jesus in a personal way, share the Good News and pray with him to surrender to Jesus. Proceed only if you feel confident he has made a sincere prayer. If you are uncertain that the person has surrendered to Jesus as his Savior and Lord, ask to lead him in a prayer of recommitment, personally acknowledging sorrow for sins and his need for the cross. Have the person ask Jesus to fill him with the Holy Spirit.

If an evil spirit has manifested, the manifestation may pinpoint the problem and allow the person to release quickly. I have seen people go through in ten minutes what may ordinarily take several hours simply because they have been touched by the Lord and are responding to Him. (When I refer to long, several-hour sessions, I am generally referring to time spent in extended interview and renunciation, rather than extended times of spiritual conflict typical to other deliverance models.)

I lead the person in a prayer of repentance for sins acknowledged in the interview and have him pronounce forgiveness to anyone not fully forgiven. (He must be willing to do so, but often heartfelt repentance and forgiveness do not take place until after renouncing the area of bondage and breaking the power⁵). Explain how the power of Jesus can be released to enable him to forgive. Have him name the person and the offense. (See chapter 4.)

Renounce Each Area of Bondage

To give up or renounce a specific area of bondage means to withdraw from any engagement, commitment, agreement or covenant the person has made with the enemy—whether physical, mental or spiritual. Have the person be specific and renounce in a clear and firm voice. If the person is too weak to express himself firmly, I generally proceed, noting that I may have to return to this issue of firm resolve. But he must speak the words the best he can.

Always have him identify with Jesus and His power by saying, "In the name of Jesus," because demons respond to Jesus, His presence and His authority expressed through us. The power is in His name. The repetition of these words drives home the fact that our liberation comes through Jesus Christ and equips the person to understand how to deal with demonic influence in the future. (One need not become legalistic about having him get every word correct.)

For example:

General areas of oppression. Have the person renounce anything from which he seeks freedom. "In the name of Jesus I renounce lust. In the name of Jesus I renounce fear." Have him renounce other spirits and lies one at a time such as unforgiveness, deception, manipulation, control, fantasy, self-pity. . . ." The list can be long.

Spiritual bondage. "In the name of Jesus I renounce the authority I gave over my life to (name of fortuneteller, soothsayer, witch, sorcerer or wizard) and to the spirit that operated in (name)."

Physical bondage. If it seems that the lack of freedom is rooted in sexual unions outside of marriage (often referred to as a soul tie), you may suggest: "In the name of Jesus I renounce all sexual and spiritual binding to (name of person), and I take back the authority I gave to him/her."

It is not necessary to distinguish between the lie and the spirit at work in the lies. I encourage the person to take his stand, renouncing all the works (lies) of the devil. I use the principle "when in doubt renounce." If it is a long list, I reassure him by telling him that most of the spirits he renounces may be insignificant, but some will be the key to his freedom. Another approach is to identify that which is being renounced as lies and deception, telling him that some of those lies may have taken a deep hold in his life. The lie and the spirit behind the lie holds him in bondage. Briefly explain that things like greed, lust, hatred and unforgiveness are all deceptions because they substitute for our wholehearted trust in the Father's provision and His limitless love for us. It is a deception that these things can protect us, provide for us or produce any good fruit in our lives. Once the authority of Jesus through the spoken word of the believer breaks the power of the lie, the spirit must leave, but it will usually linger until it is told (in the name of Jesus) to depart. Once the enemy's hold is broken, the Kingdom of God will advance, bringing healing and restoration. This means you do not have to determine prior to ministry if this is a "case for deliverance."

Pablo Bottari taught me several important things. The first is not to cast out the spirits until they are all renounced. If you cast them out one by one, you may cause greater manifestations than are necessary. If the legal right is broken, they will have to go when the ruling spirit has been renounced or the root cause has been healed. It is not necessary to try to cast them out one by one, though sometimes, after each spirit is renounced, I do break the power of the spirit in the name of

201

Jesus. This does two things: First, since the spirit has not yet been cast out it breaks the power of the spirit from interfering with further deliverance; second, my words impart courage and faith to the person who has just renounced an area of significant bondage. This can be done simply by saying, "I break this bondage in the name of Jesus." Or "I break the power of the spirit of (fear) in the name of Jesus."

After the person has renounced all the things that have been revealed in the interview, I stop and listen to the Lord; I wait. Then I may suggest a few more areas to renounce and ask if there is anything else the person would like to renounce. Sometimes the person will ask first: "Can I re- nounce _____?" "Sure, go ahead!" I tell him. Once someone senses the power of renouncing, he may want to take time to renounce many things. It is like doing a spiritual spring- cleaning, during which he may find some cobwebs that have been hidden from view.

Once the renunciation is complete, it is time to take authority.

Taking Authority

I ask the person to be quiet, and I place my hand on his head and say, "In the name of Jesus I break the power of every spirit that (name) has renounced and any related spirit, and I command them to leave now in the name of Jesus." Many variations of words can be used. I like these words because, once again, I am supporting the work of renunciation that the person has done. I am standing in a prayer of agreement. I am speaking in the name of Jesus, signifying that Jesus, the deliverer, is the One who is driving out the spirits.

Some prefer a second option—having the person himself command the spirits to leave. This further emphasizes that the person is taking responsibility for his own life by the power and authority he has in Jesus. If you do this, follow the person's command with your own command. "Again, I tell you that if two of you on earth agree about anything you ask for, it will be done for you by my Father in heaven" (Matthew 18:19). I suggest this because the afflicted person may lack faith and the experience of God's authority over the enemy. Hearing a voice of authority and sensing the response of the enemy to the name of Jesus imparts faith.

Using this second option may be important to those whose pastoral authority has restricted the ministry of deliverance, allowing only designated people to do so. If you are guiding a friend to respond to the principles in this book, you are helping that person in what could be called self-deliverance. It is unlikely that a restriction would be placed on someone who is resisting the devil and taking responsibility for his life in the name of Jesus.

Pastoral restrictions placed on who may pray for deliverance usually focus on this precise point of commanding the devil and his evil spirits to leave. This is what books and movies are made about. This is the place where in many cases the respect for the individual's dignity is lost as the confrontation with demons begins. It is right for those with spiritual authority to be concerned for the well-being of their congregations or churches under their care.

There are two types of restrictions. The first is individual. Your pastor does not want an individual serving in a particular ministry and makes it clear that he has not authorized that person to do so. It is very important that each of us is open with our pastor about what we are doing and that we are responsive to our pastor's direction.

The second type of restriction involves church guidelines, policy or directives. Due to abuses and confusion (which the devil loves), it is good to have guidelines that protect the congregation. Be respectful and patient as the Lord brings forth wisdom in the area of deliverance. Harm has been done to local churches through independent ministries that are looked upon as experts. The pastor has ongoing responsibility for the health of the congregation. The pastor or those who have been entrusted with spiritual authority are better able to judge by the fruit and discern the best way to integrate the wisdom that comes through conference speakers and trans-local ministries.[6]

I speak the word of command with my eyes open, observing what—if anything—happens. Sometimes there may be a sigh or a cough or some other expression of a spirit leaving. Sometimes you can see stress lift from a face. You may observe what can be identified as relief or peace or joy. Sometimes you will see nothing at all. Other times the internal conflict with the evil spirit will surface again.

If there is a manifestation of evil, I stop to get the person's attention and return to the interview process. I ask what the person is experiencing. Usually he can tell me something that indicates where to pick up the interview. Often renouncing and taking authority over the first set of spirits opens the door to a deeper chamber of the heart. Earlier I told you about a woman who believed her family was cursed. It was not until we commanded the spirits to leave the first time that she remembered she bought her home from a witch who had cursed all the neighbors.

Whether or not I observe evidence of deliverance or am aware that the person has been set free, I always ask, "Is anything coming to your mind? Do you feel anything?" I never tell people that they are free; that is for them to tell me. To overcome the enemy in their lives, they need to have *their* testimony, not mine.

Some might smile or laugh. Others may say, "I see a mental picture. I see fireworks." "Is that good?" I ask. "Oh, yes, it is wonderful!" Then I might share the interpretation of the picture I have received: "It is Independence Day. You are free."

Other times someone may say something that has come to his mind. A common phrase goes something like this: "I just don't think I will ever be free." This can be an expression of a spirit of doubt and unbelief, or it can reveal a spirit of hopelessness and despair. I may sense that having him renounce these spirits or others may be all that is needed; other times I return to a more extensive interview.

Depending on their culture, personality or Christian formation, some people may make no outward expression; the inward change may be unobservable. When I prayed with a group of young Haitian believers to be free from the influence of voodoo, many testified to being set free. As they were prayed for, they would say, "I felt something lift" or "I feel free," politely thanking me. I asked my interpreter if it was simply cultural to be nice and say such things. "No, they are a very spiritually sensitive people, and they would not say that if they did not know it was true." We cannot always judge with our eyes.

If It Is Clear . . .

If it is clear that the person is not free, stop and go back to the interview. This is the second thing Pablo taught me that brought such freedom in my ministry. Much that I had previously read made me think that if the person was not free by this point, a confrontation with evil spirits was at hand. But now my primary concern in a deliverance session is the interview and renunciation. *The major focus of deliverance ministry is helping the person make the proper response to the Lord as He exposes the heart.* When I am praying with someone I am teaching by example how the person may respond to the Lord on his own or with others. (This is one reason I took so much time examining the principles in the first part of this book.)

What happens if they are not free and it seems time to quit? Sometimes people just need more time for God to speak to them, to open up their hearts or to decide if they really want to be free. To step back and pray again at another time can be very helpful. This is possible if you have created the right context for deliverance, characterized by the following:

- Deliverance is something Jesus is doing; you are assisting people in their response. They can place their trust in Jesus.
- They are learning to take responsibility for their lives. You will not do it for them.
- The session is not a traumatic experience where people need to have it over and done with at all costs.

Prayer of Thanksgiving

Once someone seems to be free, lead him in a prayer of thanksgiving for deliverance: "Thank You, Jesus, for setting me free." Help him to be specific. "Thank You, Jesus, that I have forgiven my father . . . the man who abused me . . . Thank You for victory over lust . . . Thank You, Jesus, for setting me free from fear . . . Thank You that I have forgiven my uncle for molesting me." If the person is not yet free, this will expose the afflicting spirit. There is no need to torment the evil spirit by commanding it to leave. Go back to the interview and cut it off at the root through repentance, renunciation and forgiveness.

Encourage and bless what has happened. One reason I do not tell people they are free (I only confirm what they declare) is because many times they will need to go deeper. I want the experience to be characterized by the compassion of Jesus so they will not hesitate to seek further deliverance if needed.

The goal of deliverance prayer is that the person experience love and care, that he leave encouraged, trusting the Lord. I often tell people who sit in on prayer sessions with Janet and me that they can learn more in a session where the deliverance is not complete than in one that ends with a great release. If you can learn how to do well in an "incomplete" session, you will not be tempted to take too much responsibility on yourself. And, not having that pressure, you will be a better instrument of the Lord.

Blessing

Following the deliverance, pray for the person to be newly filled with the Holy Spirit; speak words of blessing and acceptance. If the house has been swept clean (Luke 11:25), then it should not be left empty, but rather filled with the light of Jesus and His presence.

If the person has not been set free, this prayer of blessing and filling may strengthen him to take the next step and deal with the things in his life that the Lord is touching. Part of the deliverance process is building up the person so that once he casts off the enemy, he can maintain and grow in freedom.

For those who have been set free, this prayer fills the emptiness that allowed the enemy to enter. The affirmation strengthens them for the battle and the plan God has for their lives.

If there is anything I wish to grow in, it is the ability to speak blessing into someone's life. I long to be able, by the power of the Spirit, to discern the area of deepest need and speak something that God sees in the person, something at the core of his being that he understands and knows but has yet to own, because it has never been spoken. As you pray for people, be open to the Holy Spirit revealing their hearts to you so you can bring blessing to their identities and destinies. Always remember the Father is passionate to bless His children. Sometimes we just have to get out of the way and ask God to speak to them.

Never Neat

One reason so many are deterred from deliverance ministry is that it is never neat. It helps if you stick to the basics and keep it simple, but it is not black and white; it is as complicated as people are. We want it to be over, yet there are always new battles to fight, something else to learn. As soon as we think we have arrived we are humbled by what we do not know.

When I was in the Ukraine I had a question-and-answer session. It seemed as if every question was a request for a formula of exactly what to do in this situation or that situation. Finally one of the local leaders stood up and spoke very strongly. Later he explained to me what I was missing.

They had grown up under Communism. Since the church had been pushed underground, the people had largely come under the influence of the occult. In the occult there is no personal responsibility; the whole objective is to get someone dependent on the healer or fortuneteller. The occult practitioner would tell the people exactly what to do, and many would do it. All of us tend to want a formula and not a relationship: "Tell me what to do." Christianity is all about a relationship with the Lord and how we express our love to Him. The practice of our faith is meant to bring us to the person of Jesus. As we are nurtured in the Church, we come to know who we are as we are joined to Jesus and receive the Father's blessing.

After receiving deliverance, Christians should receive instruction, encouragement, warning and direction to help them cooperate with the grace of God so as to remain free. Now that they have been set free, they have greater freedom to make the right choices. Now they can develop new patterns of behavior and thinking that are built daily by trusting in Jesus, making the right choices, repenting quickly and living in the light as a follower of Jesus among the fellowship of believers.

If they have not already done so, they must cleanse their homes, physically destroying anything that represents the kingdom of darkness. Anything that was used in satanic practice must be destroyed. Items that are symbols of occult activity become a connection to the spirit behind the practice.

You may have sincerely renounced the spirits afflicting you, but the continued presence of the objects connected with them stands as evidence that you have not, and the spirits may refuse to leave or, if they have left, quickly return.

Do What the Father Is Doing

We need to learn all we can so that we will not easily be deceived and we will better serve those the Lord sends to us. The foundation for all that we learn through study, from others and through our own experience is that the work of deliverance is the work of Jesus Christ. He comes by the Holy Spirit to set the captives free. We are but His instruments, seeking to love the Father's children with the love that has captured our hearts. We cannot allow our human compassion to get in the way of His compassion.

The healings recorded in John 4 and 5 illustrate that only God knows the human heart and what each person needs for healing. One story is about the healing of the son of a royal official in Herod's court. Having heard of Jesus, he walked twenty miles and humbled himself before a mere carpenter turned rabbi. He begged Jesus to come and heal his son.

Jesus challenged him: "Unless you people see miraculous signs and wonders, you will never believe" (John 4:48). This would not have been my reply. On the surface it appears rude. If this man had come to me, demonstrating such humility, I would have thought he was ready to receive from God. Evidently Jesus, who knew his heart, could see that something else was needed. Jesus tested him, as he did the Canaanite woman who begged Jesus to deliver her daughter. His first response to her was, "I was sent only to the lost sheep of Israel." His second response was, "It is not right to take the children's bread and toss it to their dogs" (Matthew 15:24–26).

Sometimes people who seem to be deeply broken, desperate and humbled have not yet been prepared by God for what

He wants to give them. Sometimes it is because they cling to an area they need to surrender to God, and they are being made ready for that moment of surrender. Other times God wants to do more in us than what we are asking for. When we pray for someone we need always to keep in mind that this is God's work; we should not create expectation for God to do things in accordance with our time. We should, like Jesus, seek to know what God is doing in one's heart.

Fortunately the royal official, like the Canaanite woman, was undeterred by Jesus' remarks. He pled with Jesus, "Sir, come down before my child dies." And Jesus told him to go home; his son would live.

I almost never tell people I think they need deliverance. The testimony of what God has done in others is enough to impart hope and courage to ask for more help. The act of asking for help is a sign that grace has been released to receive. I never want to give the appearance that their deliverance is in any way dependent on me. It is the work of God, and everything that happens in their daily lives is part of the work of God to set them free. The deliverance session is a time to process what God has done and is doing in their lives.

Another healing, in John 5, reminds me of people who come for help and have very little expectation, only to find that God has something big for them. Here an invalid for 38 years did not know Jesus or anything about Him. He was lying by a pool hoping that somehow he could get into the pool, known to be an instrument of God's healing power. But Jesus approached him and said, "Do you want to get well?" Jesus healed him; the man picked up his mat and walked away.

When people criticized Jesus for healing this man on the Sabbath, Jesus replied: "My Father is always at his work to this very day, and I, too, am working" (John 5:17). Jesus is saying, "I see something you don't see. You see a man carrying a mat on the Sabbath, but I see the demonstration of My Father's compassion and love." Jesus kept talking: "I tell you the truth, the Son can do nothing by himself; he can do only what he sees his Father doing, because whatever the Father does the Son also does" (John 5:19).

There were many people by the pool of Bethesda hoping to be healed that day. Jesus went to this man who had never heard of Him, but when a royal official traveled twenty miles and humbled himself because he believed in Jesus, he was tested. It is not easy to understand the ways of the Lord. However, it is our responsibility to follow and obey. It is very difficult to see those we love, those who are desperate to be set free, still struggling to receive their deliverance. We must look to Jesus as our model and say with Him, "I can do nothing by myself; I can do only what I see the Father doing."

> "A new command I give you: Love one another. As I have loved, so you must love one another."
>
> *John 13:34*

Lord, You loved me by becoming like me in all things but sin. You called me by name and gave me hope. As You have loved me may I love those you send to me. Yes, I believe that You can use me as an instrument of Your love, as Your servant.

Evil spirits want to produce fear and draw attention to themselves through manifestations. The next chapter will help you understand why there is no need to be afraid and how manifestations can be reduced.

14

How to Handle Manifestations

> It makes me angry that we have to do this, defend ourselves
> against people who won't show their face.
>
> Marie Forkin, a young mother of two,
aboard the USS Roosevelt on an indefinite tour
of duty fighting the war on terrorism

Stories abound about very significant exorcisms happening today. As a result many have been awakened to the reality of the devil's work in the lives of believers. Satan, as part of a strategy to turn his defeats into victories, can exploit this focus on evil manifestations. If he can get us to focus on the most radical cases, provoking fear, he can continue to hide his strategies in the lives of everyday believers.

In the first part of this book, I focused on the person and avoided discussion of manifestations (even though I probably would sell more books if I did the opposite). Yet if we do not know how to respond to a manifestation of evil, we may be subject to fear, which drives away love. Here I discuss manifestations more thoroughly, in the context of praying for deliverance with someone.

Manifestations of evil spirits may prompt someone to seek help. They may be evident from the start. In other cases, someone may manifest an evil spirit in the course of deliverance. This chapter applies to both cases.

Five years ago, Carlos Annacondia came from Argentina to do a crusade in Philadelphia. For more than thirty years Carlos has led large crusades, often focusing on the poorest of the poor, the most afflicted members of society. The message he brought to us was that we cannot just introduce people to salvation in Christ; we need to see them liberated from bondage so they can follow through on their commitment. His book *Listen to Me, Satan* is titled after the word of command he speaks after people have come forward and prayed to yield their lives to God. "Listen to me, Satan" is followed by "in the name of Jesus Christ. . . ."

At the time, the thought of someone commanding Satan to listen to him in the midst of thousands of people seemed a bit wild to me. The manifestations, the potential for psychological manipulation, the harm that could be done to people as demons were exposed that they were not ready to release—not to mention my own fears of being out of control and what I now recognize as an unconfessed fear of the devil—all made me a bit cautious.

Fortunately I had already met Pablo Bottari. As I mentioned, Pablo was in charge of the "deliverance tent"—the place where all those who manifested evil spirits during the crusade were taken. Pablo had come the previous year to Philadelphia and taught on deliverance ministry. Some of the things he taught me enabled me to resume ministry after I had backed away from it for years. But more important than teaching me, Pablo prayed with me. He looked into my eyes and said, "You are a lover of souls." I knew what he meant. I have always been concerned about the things of the heart, the inner things, the hidden things that keep us from full freedom in Christ. I had written a book about getting free from the sins of the heart. The mark of Pablo's ministry is

213

love and kindness to people and treating them with respect. He saw something in me and invested in me. Now Carlos Annacondia was coming, and I was asked to train people and help organize the deliverance tent.

Close to three hundred people came to the training. At the crusade, hundreds of people were brought to the deliverance tent to be prayed with, and I have heard no negative reports from these folks. Many were set free of bondage. Many more felt loved and cared for.

I am not sure Carlos's style would work in every culture the way it does in Argentina. But I did learn some valuable lessons from him.

First, if you are prepared to care for people, there is no need to be afraid of manifestations of evil. What Carlos was doing was very similar (but in a very different context) to what was done in the third and fourth centuries. Accounts from these early Church times detail how new Christians preparing for baptism over a three-year period were prayed with for deliverance from evil spirits. These exorcisms were a part of their preparation. On the final week they were prayed with intensely for many hours a day to be set free. The bishop came to pray for the baptism candidates during the last week before baptism. The prayer served to make manifest any spirit hidden in darkness, because any hidden bondage would threaten the individual's relationship with the Lord and the unity of the local church. The believers were not afraid because they knew how to deal with demons that manifested. Deliverance was a normal part of the formation process for new believers.

Second, if you are not afraid of the devil and you express such, faith will rise up in those who are afflicted and they will put aside their fears and come to Jesus for help. Understanding reduces fear. One reason I wrote this book is so that those seeking deliverance will understand how to cooperate with the Holy Spirit both before and after the prayer session.

Three Steps

From Pablo Bottari I learned four steps for dealing with manifestations of evil. These are explained more fully in his book *Free in Christ* (Creation House).

Make sure this is really a manifestation of an evil spirit

The word *manifest* simply means something is made visible. For example, a physical manifestation of evil spirits may mean a person loses control over his body, his face becomes twisted, his eyes become glassy and the person no longer seems to be present. In more severe episodes the spirits seizes control and the person becomes so submerged that in a sense he loses consciousness. (I like the term "temporary possession" that Francis MacNutt uses to describe such manifestations.) In a situation like this the person may not remember anything that happens during the session. He may emerge bewildered and frightened and needs to be greeted by reassurance, acceptance and love.

As you evaluate, consider whether what looks to be a manifestation of evil might be something else. It could, for example, be an unusual emotional reaction to the love of God or some ongoing psychological condition (which may have a physiological basis). It may be an adverse reaction to medication. It is important to take the person to a private place where he can feel safe during the deliverance process.

Stop and ask yourself what you see. Is there an expression of torment, fear, anger, shame or sensuality? Discernment is a gift that grows with experience. Trust that God will allow you to grow in discernment, make note of your impressions and use them to influence your interview.

Although it is best to pray for deliverance with a minimum of manifestations, we can rejoice when the enemy has been exposed and is no longer hidden. If the Kingdom of God is revealed, the enemy may manifest in the same ways we read about in the New Testament (see Mark 1:26; Mark 9:20; Luke 8:29). God, in His mercy, may reveal to someone what the spirits he has yielded to are really like. There is nothing like a manifestation of evil to convince someone to get out of spiritism, stop channeling or leave voodoo.

Take authority over the devil in a simple and firm way

In Luke 10:17 we are told that the 72 returned with joy and said, "Lord, even the demons submit to us in your name." A simple way to take authority is to say firmly, "Submit yourself in the name of Jesus." Be careful that you don't give the impression that you are taking authority over the person. You also don't want to frighten the person in any way.

Act immediately on the authority you have taken

You do not have to repeat the command. Just exercise your faith. Have the person open his eyes. Help him regain control over himself and give you his attention. Talk to the person, smile at him and verbally express the compassion of Jesus. Help him feel safe. If you are at peace, he will relax.

If it is a difficult case, you may speak to the person firmly by name and say something like, "Ann, take control of your body and your mind in the name of Jesus. Open your eyes." Knowing and speaking the person's name is very helpful.

Do not command the spirits to leave. Do not keep binding the spirits. Keep speaking to the person in love. You can say, "Ann, I want to speak to you. Jesus loves you, and there are people here who love you. I do not want to talk to any demon. I want to talk to you. Can you help me? We want to help you. Look at me, Ann."

Someone may be shocked to have what seems like a "friendly" spirit exposed as evil. When I was a young and ignorant believer, I visited a friend in England. His girlfriend and he regularly held séances, supposedly to bring back her dead sister. *Why not?* I thought, foolishly. Fortunately I did have one sensible thought. I blessed myself, saying, "What I do, I do in the name of the Father and the Son and the Holy Spirit." As soon as they put their hands on the glass, it shot out from under them. Fright came to their faces. "That thing is evil," my friend declared. They would not go back to it that night; they were shaken by what they felt.

Seek to understand the person

People who manifest the presence of an evil spirit may have a variety of things going on. They may be unfamiliar with manifestations and feel petrified, thinking they are out of control. They might feel fear or embarrassment. We need to address their fears as we speak to them in love. Other times people feel relief that their problem is out in the open. It is no longer hidden. They are relieved to know the source of their compulsions. Or they could be expressing deep emotional pain and find relief in doing so. We need to help them process the pain that has surfaced.

Sometimes people have a subtle desire for evil spirits to manifest, or they think that yielding to the manifestation will help them be delivered of the evil spirit. They may think, "Finally my enemy is exposed; I don't want him to hide again."

Manifestations are good if they are provoked by the Spirit of God, exposing the works of darkness. They may help someone find the courage to touch the deep, hidden places of the soul. This is true especially if someone is present to help the person find liberty. It may not be good if all they are doing is manifesting the darkness and not receiving proper pastoral care.

It is actually easier to help someone if he has manifested. It means the area Jesus is dealing with has come to the surface. Understanding what to do if there is a manifestation robs the devil of one of his tactics: intimidation.

217

Once we understand manifestations of evil and how to help a person who is experiencing them, there is no need to be afraid. Manifestations do not need to be provoked to help someone find deliverance. One rule of thumb is that if you expect manifestations, you will probably see them. But if you don't expect them and you avoid provoking them, manifestations can be significantly reduced. A minister brought a twenty-year-old woman who had been manifesting continually during several sessions in which he had prayed a prayer of exorcism. She had been abandoned to an orphanage at birth and then retrieved for visits by her mentally ill father, who had raped her when she was three. I had no expectation for manifestations to occur. Using the principles in this book, she experienced release with no further disturbance. The attitude of the prayer leader may be the critical factor.

One of my desires is to reduce unnecessary manifestations for the sake of the person for whom I am praying (also because unnecessary manifestations contribute to the resistance many Christians have toward deliverance). But a fear of manifestations or a desire to control the process of deliverance will be a hindrance. Usually a manifestation is a sign of conflict that needs to be resolved, but other times it is an expression of release that should not be hindered. Discernment grows with experience.

Chapter 15 includes two extended stories of deliverance, one involving manifestations and the other not. These anecdotes illustrate the importance of understanding personal dynamics, listening to the person and to the Holy Spirit, and working to bring freedom at increasingly deeper levels of the heart.

"And now, O LORD my God, thou hast made thy servant king instead of David my father: and I am but a little child: I do not know how to go out or come in.". . . [It] pleased the LORD, that Solomon had asked this.

I Kings 3:7, 10

Lord, Solomon asked for the gift of understanding so that he could discern between good and evil. He knew he was not up to the task. But You were pleased to give him wisdom. I, too, ask for wisdom for I am like that little child and do not know when to go out or come in.

Everyone who experiences deliverance from bondage has a story worth telling. It is the account of God's redeeming love manifested in one's life. The final chapter contains two stories that demonstrate the love of God releasing the gift of hope.

15

Ongoing Deliverance

> For transfiguration is not something we can achieve; it is something which only he who is mighty can bring about in us.
>
> Gerald Vann

I would like to conclude by sharing with you two cases where I applied the principles of this book. Many examples in this book are simple cases of liberation from evil spirits. These stories are more involved. I include them here for three reasons. First, they illustrate how the principles are applied in very different situations (with and without physical manifestations). Second, they demonstrate how deliverance can come at deeper and deeper levels. Third, they offer a message of hope for those who are deeply afflicted.

Kevin's Story

Queer, fag, weirdo, sissy. Kevin heard these words for years, from grade school through high school. It was hurtful and confusing, and over time he learned to detach from his emotions.

Although he had friends who were girls, he felt isolated from "the guys." Part of this was due to the fact that he was more sensitive and emotionally expressive than his peers. Although he was not effeminate, even a natural athlete, he was vulnerable to the taunts from other boys. But part of his isolation stemmed from something deeper he had yet to discover.

The summer before his freshman year in high school, Kevin read in the newspaper about a section of his city where gay men went looking for sex. Curiosity and the need for affection led him to travel by himself to that area. It did not take long before he found himself in the utility closet of a parking garage with a man in his late twenties. This was his introduction to anonymous sex. From the beginning he was very passive, allowing things to be done to him and then following the lead. He came home after that first night feeling dirty, but also excited. For three years he returned, sometimes three or four times per week. He never considered that older men were abusing him, because he chose to go. In spite of his activity, Kevin also had a desire to be married and have children. In his twisted thinking, he thought that sex with a woman was reserved for after marriage, and he wanted to wait. Until then, men were for sex.

At seventeen, he began to think about college and his future. "I could never fool a woman into marrying me if I continue to live this way," he thought. He broke the pattern. In college he made many friends and a new life, distracted from his old ways. After college, at 24, he became a committed Christian. He then began to face and deal with his issues, going regularly to counseling. During the next five years he acted out three times, repenting quickly each time; but he was not free.

Breaking the Oppression

At thirty, Kevin married Sarah, a wonderful Christian woman with whom he had shared his story. Together they would face the testing of Kevin's new commitment. A year and a half later, now struggling with Internet pornography and under high stress, Kevin again engaged in homosexual sex, opening himself, and consequently his wife, to the risk of HIV. They were both devastated. Sarah went to be with her mom. Kevin was petrified that he would be abandoned and everything he loved would be lost. However his wife forgave him and came home. This is when Kevin first came for deliverance prayer. He confessed everything, renounced everything, forgave everyone; he was desperate.

After two sessions he felt free. "It was amazing," he said. "For a year and a half I did not look at men with lust. There was no masturbation, no pornography. I could see a man's body, look at skin and not be lustful. There was such a radical change in me." Even an old habit of picking his lip until it bled went away.

But over the next eighteen months he hit a downward spiral. He struggled in prayer. Anxiety returned as his family grew. Then masturbation. Then pornography. Then it all returned. The last thing to return was the habit of picking his lip.

Going Deeper

Kevin came back for help. This time, he went deeper in his forgiveness, specifically of his dad. Few people have as many images in prayer as Kevin does. For him, they act as a record of what was going on in him as we prayed. But this is not necessary for healing or deliverance.

During prayer Kevin had a picture of standing in his mom's bedroom, with her sitting on the bed holding his sister. As he pictured his dad come into the room, he saw what seemed like spears and daggers of rage come out of his mom. They spread like the tail of a peacock and stood between him and his dad. He wanted but could not get to his dad. If he tried, the blades would destroy him. As we prayed for the Lord to enter the scene with His truth, Kevin pictured Jesus walk into the room and then into his dad and become one with him. Immediately the blades and spears disappeared and Kevin saw himself jump into his dad's arms. Kevin's reflected that something in or from his mom was separating him from his dad. He felt that deep down, when he was very young, he made a choice. Due to his perception at the time, he felt he had to choose his mom and pull back from his dad.

"I was too fearful to choose Dad," he recalls. How unfortunate that he needed to make a choice! Recently he told me, "From that prayer till this day, I feel as though I continue to connect with my father and all the good things that he did. . . . Now my heart is filled with gratitude for him."

This gave Kevin temporary relief. Something deeper still needed to be touched. The day came when he placed himself in a situation of temptation again. A man approached him and they began to talk. He realized what was about to happen, and at the last moment he fled. He came back once again asking for help and later wrote in his journal: "I can't believe it had to take a fall—or at least a very close call—to get me to the point of surrendering again. . . . Neal specifically spoke to me about pride in my Christianity, that somehow I was proud about being a Christian and used it to take a position of superiority. It was true. Neal led me to renounce fears of isolation, rejection, condemnation, superiority, anger and others. A number of things happened that night, but the bottom line is that I realized that, although I may have surrendered my life once or twice to the Lord before, I never really honored Him as my 'Lord.' . . . Since that prayer, I now start out my times of prayer on my knees recognizing how much greater He is than I."

The Root

When we got together for the next session, I felt the Lord say to me, "False identity." I waited to see what this meant.

As we prayed, the forgiveness toward his mother went much deeper—forgiveness for situations and words that expressed control, disapproval and rejection. I felt as though the foundation was healed and now the spirit behind homosexuality had to be renounced. After Kevin renounced it I commanded it to leave. I could feel it lift off of him. "What is going on?" I asked.

"I see this large truck leaving the docks," he said. Later in his journal, he wrote that he felt sadness "that an old friend, or at least a longtime acquaintance" was leaving. "I turned around with a sigh, wiped my hands, and wondered 'What's next?' as I looked at the huge, now empty warehouse of my soul, life and identity. Suddenly people and angels started filing into the warehouse, greeting me, getting to work straightening up and starting to rebuild. It was as if they were always there, just hidden or covered. Neal prayed that the body, the Church, would surround me and restore me."

The next day Kevin wrote: "Aside from fairly mild symptoms of anxiety, I feel like a new man today. Deep down I know something is very different, very new. I have a new hope. . . . At church this morning . . . I had an overwhelming sense that I was small and God was huge, and He was blessing me with a deeper appreciation of that fact."

Three days later he wrote: "God is showing me the depth of the depravity of my sin. I am remembering and seeing some of the wicked things I have done throughout my life, realizing, in spite of my pleasantness and niceness, that I have been a major sinner, so much more than I have ever admitted. I have worked so hard all my life to create an image of being strong and self-sufficient; it is all a facade that has come crumbling down. Lord, give me the grace to walk away from the broken idol of myself that I have created." Kevin was given the gift of repentance.

One morning in prayer Kevin remembered being picked on in grade school. He felt the hurt in a deep way and offered his "bruised heart" to the Lord.

Taking It Back

That night I prayed with Kevin. The next morning he wrote:

"More deliverance prayer last night, specifically praying about being teased when I was in fourth and fifth grades. I renounced spirits of rejection, abandonment, isolation and hurt; I forgave the boys that picked on me, specifically naming them and the names they called me. As we renounced and broke the power of the spirits, I saw myself as a boy walking up the path to school. I was afraid to go because I was afraid of being attacked, as if I were walking through a forest and there was something hiding behind every tree. As I went through the process of renouncing and forgiving, I experienced greater freedom as I continued picturing myself walking that same path to school, each time with greater freedom. But each time I saw myself on that path, I was not getting closer to the school. I felt as if I was closer to my home. This part of the prayer was very difficult; it felt as though nothing was happening. Twice I almost gave up (Neal said he was strongly tempted to give up at this point, too), but then Neal had me renounce fear and sadness. In my vision, I remembered that I had left something at home. I didn't know what it was, but I knew that Mom was holding it. I pictured myself going home to get it. It was silver and ornate, but I still wasn't sure what it was. I was afraid to take it from her. Even asking Jesus to help me, I could not take it. Neal asked me, 'What would your mom do if you took it?' I said, 'She would either fall apart or get angry.' Neal led me to renounce fear of anger, fear of criticism, fear of abandonment and fear of rejection. After Neal commanded them to leave I could see myself yelling, 'Give it to me! It is mine!' Finally with the Lord's help, I had it. I then pictured myself sitting on the floor (Mom wasn't in the picture anymore) holding this thing. I was small and a little disfigured. Neal prayed that the Lord would put it in me because I knew that's where it belonged. When he placed his hand on my chest, I could sense the Lord putting it in me. As it entered, I felt like I grew and began to take shape as a boy,

225

but I was shining like silver or gold, like a trophy. That silver thing was me! It was my boyhood! It was my identity! I'd been missing it all my life. Suddenly, I could see myself jump up, now dressed in a baseball uniform, and with excitement, joy and enthusiasm running off. I saw myself calling out to the guys who had picked on me, 'Wait up! Here I come,' knowing they were just waiting for me, that they accepted me. I wasn't afraid. It was as if they were waiting for the whole 'me' the entire time. The reason they picked on me was because I never showed them the whole real me, and they somehow knew that. The whole me wasn't there and they picked on the incomplete picture that I offered them. I felt like I was growing into a man; that this healing wasn't just for the boy in me, it was for all of me. I felt myself grow and mature in strength, even in physical size."

When I placed my hand on Kevin's chest and prayed that he would receive what was his, he rose up in his seat as he felt it enter him. Afterward, he looked down at his arms and said, "Wow! I feel buff!" Years earlier Kevin had worked hard in the gym, building his body. When he was drawn to pornography he was drawn to the skin, especially a man's physique. He was looking for something that he thought he was lacking. Now he found what he was searching for—he received the freedom to embrace his manhood.

That day his journal entry ended with: "Thank You, Lord, for creating me! For forgiving me . . . for giving me shape and form, for being with me all of my life! Thank You for helping me find myself, my identity. You are faithful, loving and awesome!"

One Year Later

One year later Kevin was walking in freedom, knowing he would never be the same again. He had many opportunities to help others with similar problems. Then he began to slip: walking in parks that reminded him of how he used to find comfort in sin; dabbling on the Internet, looking for pictures of "fit" men. Pornography was the next step. Tormented, he confessed his sin openly, and we prayed for him briefly several times. Each time he experienced relief and renewed hope.

One day the urgent call came: "I need help. I feel like I'm an addict again." Janet and I prayed as we waited in the living room for Kevin and Sarah to put the children to bed. "Lord, is this a lack of willpower, the power of sin, old thought patterns resurfacing, a final attempt by the enemy to regain control? Or are You after something deeper?" I prayed. "Please lead us and reveal what is hidden."

"Dad, Dad, Dad," Kevin's son called from the steps, inter-rupting as we were about to begin. I wrote on my pad at the top: "Dad, Dad, Dad."

Kevin pleaded, "I feel helpless, like God's grace is no longer present; it was so easy, I was free. Now it seems like it is 'just me' trying to do it, and I can't." We tried to help him see the lie: he was not alone, God had not abandoned him and God's grace was sufficient. We spoke at length about repentance and confession and the urgency of the situation, which required discipline and accountability. Then we prayed.

In prayer Kevin humbled himself before the Lord, seek-ing mercy and forgiveness. Then I had him renounce some things—old things like abandonment, rejection and fear. There was seemingly no response. "Dad, Dad, Dad" came to my mind. "Kevin, renounce 'fatherlessness' in the name of Jesus," I urged.

Before he could speak the words his emotions broke loose, with a gut-wrenching moan and tears. The lifelong pain of not really knowing his father was being touched and released. Once he renounced it and commanded it to depart, a flood of wonderful memories of his dad filled his mind and heart. He received a sense of his father's approval, affirmation and love, followed by a sense of letting go of his dad and embracing his destiny. God the Father was revealing His heart to Kevin.

Kevin is standing in his freedom today, confident that he will not need to return to the lies, which held him bound.

Let me summarize Kevin's journey. The roots of his addictions were found in the confusion over his identity and complicated by his sin. First, one level of oppression was broken and a process of healing and deeper deliverance began. God led Kevin to: a deeper surrender to the Lord; healing of root identity issues; deeper repentance; forgiveness; embracing his manhood; and finally a revelation of God the Father. Each victory along the way released hope and an expectation of grace for the next step. Without the follow-through Kevin may have been left greatly troubled and disillusioned, wondering why the initial deliverance "did not stick."

Kevin experienced extreme torment and moral crisis due to the deep-rooted confusion about his sexual identity and the consequences of his past sin. His journey of discovering the depth of freedom he had been given in Jesus Christ is not unusual. All of us as believers have been invited into an ongoing process of transformation, as the Holy Spirit works in our lives to make us more like Jesus.

Deborah's Story

"I should have killed you the day you were born, the way I killed the other children." A fact or not, this is what Deborah heard from her mother as she grew up. On his deathbed, her father cursed her and yelled, "Get her out of here!" In grade school she was so severely berated that she had an out-of-body experience to escape the emotional pain. From that point she felt as though she became another Deborah. In her teenage years school officials disciplined her by forcing her to stay with pigs for three days. Three different men who should have represented the love of God molested and raped her. She had been exposed to the occult through her mother, and a gypsy cursed her as an unborn baby in her mother's womb. Deborah escaped to the woods and related to a world of being friends with the animals. She could trust animals but not humans; animals were kind and loving.

No wonder that when we met Deborah she was severely demonized. It was our first seminar on deliverance and intercession. Being in another country, I felt very unsupported because the man who invited us to speak had to leave the seminar unexpectedly. The last thing I wanted was to start prayer with someone as severely troubled as Deborah. She barely got to the front of the room when her eyes became glassy and childlike fear covered her face. She was led to another room along with a number of others. I prayed with several others and saw them liberated rather quickly. Janet, in her compassion, went right to Deborah, whom she found huddled on the floor in a fetal position.

I prayed, "Lord what should we do? Should we pray for her? Is this a case to be referred to others?" When I joined Janet, Deborah was quite afraid of me. It took some time for her to open up to me as she had with Janet. After Janet related some of Deborah's story I asked, "Have you committed your life to Jesus?" Yes, she nodded. "Let's repeat the prayer. Lord Jesus, thank You for dying for me . . . Please forgive me . . . I choose to follow You as my Lord . . . Please fill me with Your Spirit." Each word was a struggle. As she tried to say the words she began to lose consciousness. "Deborah, look at me; I want to talk to you," I said. "Do you want to be free?" Yes, she responded. "Then say, 'Lord Jesus' . . . you can do it, Deborah; the Lord is with you. You need to choose to be under His authority. We cannot do it for you. If you cannot pray this prayer we will have to find someone else to help you." It took some time, but she completed the prayer.

She looked up, and we saw her beautiful smile for the first time. Then we started a process of forgiving. Each step of the way the demons wanted to take over her mind and render her mute. "Deborah, look at me," I demanded. "Stay with me and say, 'I forgive. . . .'" Repeatedly I explained that as she decided to forgive, God would do the work in her heart. When she seemed to waver I asked, "Do you want to be free?" To this she would look up with pleading eyes saying, "Yes, yes."

Freedom at Last

We led Deborah to renounce spirits of rejection, abandonment, fear—spirits that related to what she revealed in the interview. We brought her to a place of peace and promised to pray with her again. She left encouraged, having developed a special bond with Janet and receiving a gift of hope. We had two more sessions that week. Each session revealed deeper and deeper levels of pain. The time during the conference between sessions allowed her to grow stronger and prepare to go deeper.

At one point when she began to speak, I thought it was a demon, and I told it to stop. "Deborah, I want to talk to you, not the demon," I said. Then I realized God was revealing something to her. She told us about a woman who had put a curse on her. After we broke its power and told the demon to leave (in the name of Jesus), she felt relief and freedom. I suspected that if we pressed we would uncover more. But she felt free and was able to receive love from many people as the week continued. That was what she needed most. She needed to receive love. She could begin to let others in. Her complete deliverance rested with God, not me. What a joy it was to see her smile the rest of the week!

Under It and Over It Again

Deborah was free for six months. Then we got the report that she reverted. At a lonely time she pulled back into the dark world she had escaped from. The priest who led the community she belonged to had tried praying with her several times, but with little effect. He later applied to the bishop to be nominated exorcist so that he could continue to pray for Deborah.

We saw her again the following summer at another conference. Two things had happened. Her time with the exorcist had been a disaster. She would manifest and throw chairs around the room. Those assisting the exorcist held her down and twisted her arm. She left the sessions bruised. She believed the priest was angry with her and blamed her for not cooperating. She nearly choked when they poured holy water down her throat. The other thing that happened is that she met Father John. He didn't know much about deliverance prayer, but he sure understood about love. This man loved her and accepted her. He became a father to her and spent a great deal of time with her. He gave her a cell phone so she could call him at any time. Sometimes she would blank out and roam the streets of the city all night, and in the morning not know where she had been. Coming back from one of these nights, she might have a satanic symbol or book with her. The first time we ministered to her she did not get adequate follow-up support. Now she had Father John.

During the conference we had three more sessions with Deborah. This time I was able to minister to her directly, a significant step considering the way other men had misrepresented God to her. After the last session she spontaneously sang songs of deliverance as we knelt before the Lord, weeping in thanksgiving. The key this time was discovering the lie. She was convinced that no one could love her, and she would have to beg for love the rest of her life. When this lie was addressed directly, its power was broken. We gave her very detailed instructions on how to keep her freedom and related this all to Father John.

Satan did not want to let her go. The battle to stay free began immediately. The day she left the conference, he tried to intimidate her. A stranger came up to her at the train station and said, "The demons are not far from you; they are in me."

Three months later, when she went by herself to the house of her deceased parents, she looked through an old chest and found an occult object. As she picked it up she fell to the floor for several hours in a trancelike state. Finally Father John got her on the cell phone and talked her through the ordeal. (Later he came back with her, found the object and destroyed it.)

A Final Encounter

Once again we returned to Deborah's country the following year, anxious to see her. We knew she had not followed our instructions. We did not know if she had enough support. Did we do what Jesus wanted us to do? Did we cause pain? Did we love with the love of God? Should we pray with her again? "Lord, show us what to do," we pleaded.

Deborah came to the seminar again. She did not come asking for prayer; she just wanted to see us. Through it all she knew we loved her. The first year she developed a special relationship with Janet, and Janet blessed her as a mother. The next year she trusted me as a father in the Lord and allowed me to bless her. Deborah's coming to see us was my answer. We had done our job—she knew we loved her.

She was not sure she wanted prayer. For one, she kept having a disturbing memory of the exorcism she went through. In her memory she was outside her body watching herself slither on the floor like a snake. That was not her experience with us, but it remained a hindrance to more prayer. Another reason was the fact that she could not understand why so many sessions were necessary, and she was discouraged. She blamed herself and thought perhaps she was schizophrenic.

We offered to pray for her, but it needed to be her decision. The ultimate responsibility for her freedom rested with her. We waited and prayed. Toward the end of the week she did ask for prayer and even expressed anger when her appointment was delayed. This was a good sign! The anger proved that she was not "begging" for love, as the enemy had always told her.

In a session on the last day, a deeper lie was exposed: the belief that she had no heart (that Satan had eaten her heart). Satan wanted to rob her of knowing the love of God and the love that others had for her. She embraced it with her mind but was robbed of an inner knowing, which is the gift of God. The enemy's power was broken when Deborah, with great difficulty, said, "Lord Jesus, please give me a new heart." She began to cough and was free.

We prayed for the filling of the Holy Spirit and blessings upon her life. We know she is one who will love and serve others in a mighty way.

The Process of Deliverance

Deliverance is a mixture of spiritual, emotional and psychological issues. The process of deliverance can be just as important to restoring the individual as driving out the spirit is. Once the lie has been exposed, the systems of thinking that have protected the lie must be redeemed (see Romans 12:1–3). Deborah needed a safe place where she knew she was loved so she could enter more fully into the process of transformation. Without the support of Father John and others, the prayers of deliverance may have been fruitless.

In Matthew 13:24–25 Jesus tells a parable of a man who sows wheat in his field. "But while everyone was sleeping, his enemy came and sowed weeds among the wheat, and went away." If we are not alert, the enemy will sow weeds in with the wheat of deliverance so that even if the person gets free there may be weeds to deal with at another time. We cannot eliminate the weeds, but we can be alert and do our best to reduce them.

One Final Thought

The disciples had great success casting out demons as they proclaimed the Kingdom of God. In Luke 10:17 we are told: "The seventy-two returned with joy and said, 'Lord, even the demons submit to us in your name.'"

But there were other days. We are told of a father who brought his son possessed by an evil spirit to the disciples, and they could not drive it out. Jesus declared, "Everything is possible for him who believes." Then He drove the spirit out. "After Jesus had gone indoors, his disciples asked him privately, 'Why couldn't we drive it out?' He replied, 'This kind can come out only by prayer'" (Mark 9:28–29). As soon as you think you have deliverance figured out, as soon as you grow confident in your experience, something will come your way to teach you to get back on your knees and cry out desperately to God, confessing that Jesus alone is the One who sets the captives free and thanking Him for the privilege of sharing in His mission. And in our weakness we cry out as the father of the boy did: "I do believe; help me overcome my unbelief!" (Mark 9:24).

Epilogue

Christian Hope

Even if all the forces of Darkness appear to prevail, those who believe in God know that evil and death do not have the final say. Christian hope is based on this truth.

John Paul II to the American people,
September 12, 2001

September 11, 2001, we watched with horror the image of people running down the streets of New York City with a cloud of death chasing them, seeking to engulf them in its darkness. Later we saw a photograph taken of the smoke coming from the World Trade Center moments after the planes struck. In the smoke an image of an evil face emerged, captured on film. Evil was manifest. Satan's work was on display for the entire world to see. Evil remains hidden beneath the surface of the images we present to others, hidden in rationalizations and deception—evil that dwells in injustice, poverty and materialism; evil that nourishes itself in the lives of broken families and abandoned children; evil that celebrates the world of addictions and self-destruction.

Soon we were given a gift—two more images to overshadow the first. After assisting in the late-night removal of several bodies, a fireman raised his floodlight to discover a steel cross rising from the rubble. Long after the smoke and debris are removed the cross will stand. The cross points to our redemption and hope. It reminds us of the story of our salvation. We also saw the many faces of heroes who gave their lives helping others and those who bravely mourned the dead and faced an unknown future. These were the images that will leave a lasting legacy of hope.

On September 11, the world was confronted with the reality of evil. The devil is real, but without our cooperation he is no more than smoke. The work of the Redeemer is stronger than steel and is manifest in the lives of those who have chosen Him.

Christian hope is the confident expectation for good. God brings good out of evil, and the ultimate good that has been presented to us is Jesus Christ. One day we will spend eternity with our Lord Jesus Christ, to the glory of God the Father.

I began this book by telling you about Anna, who declared, "Now I have hope," as she said good-bye to us. Developing the virtue of Christian hope takes a lifetime. In our joys and trials we grow in hope as we face basic questions of life and faith.

Do I really believe there is a God who is able to help?

Do I believe He loves me, knows me and wants to help?

Do I believe there is a purpose to my life and meaning in my trials and disappointments?

Do I believe I can do something that will make a difference?

These questions start when we are young and come up again and again throughout life.

Playing in a closet when I was three years old, I pulled the door closed and found myself in total darkness. Reaching out

I realized there was no handle on the inside. I was trapped. My mom and sister were in the basement ironing. I yelled for help, but there was no response. Then I sat down among the shoes and wondered how long it would take for me to die. This is an early memory etched in my mind. How long did it take for me to resolve I was going to die? Perhaps sixty seconds. (My mother rescued me shortly after I surrendered to despair.)

The tentacles of hopelessness seek to hold our lives (or pockets of our lives) in bondage by convincing us there is no way out. We develop patterns of thinking such as, "There is no one who can help. I can never change. The problem I have is too big. I've tried everything, and I can't do anything about it." *Many fail to grow in hope because they do nothing.* It is my hope that you are now more confident that you can cooperate with the Lord as He seeks to bring you to greater liberty.

A hero is someone who does the right thing, despite his fear or personal risk. Heroes get up when they have fallen, reaffirm their confidence in God's love and move on. All heroes are tested. The greatest things in life are done by ordinary people, not because they feel like it, but because it needs to be done.

The ultimate purpose of our freedom from evil spirits is not that we would feel better but that we would surrender more fully to the Lord and give our life for the purpose of advancing the Kingdom of God.

Pray then as Jesus taught us: "Our Father who art in heaven, hallowed be thy name. Thy kingdom come. Thy will be done, on earth as it is in heaven. And lead us not into temptation, but deliver us from evil" (Matthew 6:9–10,13, RSV).

To him who is able to keep you from falling and to present you before his glorious presence without fault and with great joy—to the only God our Savior be glory, majesty, power and authority, through Jesus Christ our Lord, before all ages, now and forevermore! Amen (see Jude 1:24–25).

Appendix 1

Deliverance Questionnaire

There are many questions you may wish to ask. The list below focuses on revealing any occult connection. These questions can help provide important information quickly. You may wish to include more questions about trauma, abuse or family dysfunction.

The following is a sample taken from *Deliverance from Evil Spirits* by Francis MacNutt (Chosen Books), pp. 163–64.

Have you ever, just for fun, out of curiosity or in earnest:

1. Had your fortune told by tea leaves, palm reading, a crystal ball, etc.?
2. Read or followed horoscopes or had a chart made for you?
3. Practiced yoga or Transcendental Meditation?
4. Attended a séance or spiritualist meeting?
5. Had a reincarnation reading about who you were in some previous existence?
6. Played with an Ouija board, tarot cards or Dungeons & Dragons?

7. Played games of an occult nature using ESP, telepathy, etc.?
8. Consulted a medium, acted as a medium or practiced channeling?
9. Sought psychic healing or had psychic surgery?
10. Practiced table-lifting, lifting bodies, automatic writing or soul travel?
11. Used any kind of charm for protection?
12. Practiced water-witching to find out where to dig a well?
13. Read or possessed books on witchcraft, fortune-telling, ESP, psychic phenomena or possession? Had anything in your home that was given to you by someone in the occult?
14. Been fascinated by demonic topics in movies? Had a fascination with the occult?
15. Accepted the writings of Edgar Cayce or any other New Age author?
16. Practiced mind control over anyone, cast a magic spell or sought a psychic experience? Contacted a psychic in person or through a psychic hotline?
17. Made a pact with Satan or been involved in Satan worship?
18. Attended witchcraft or voodoo ceremonies?
19. Known of any relatives or ancestors who have been involved in witchcraft, pagan religions, fortune-telling or who have used magic spells?
20. Visited a shrine or temple of a non-Judeo-Christian religion?
21. Been involved in Freemasonry? Had anyone in your family involved?
22. Embraced the fallacy that we are self-sufficient and do not need God?
23. Used LSD, marijuana, cocaine or any "mind-expanding" drugs?

24. Had a problem with alcohol? How about other family members?
25. Exposed yourself to pornography in magazines [or the Internet], TV or stage shows, books, topless bars or X-rated movies?
26. Had a problem with habitual masturbation?
27. Been involved in sexually deviant practices?
28. Been involved with a number of people sexually?
29. Had an abortion or fathered a child who was aborted?
30. Wished yourself dead?
31. Wished somebody else dead?
32. Attempted to take your own life?
33. Attempted to take (or have taken) someone else's life?

In using such a questionnaire, we must realize that some activities (such as playing the Ouija board) are clearly forbidden, while others may involve extenuating circumstances.

Appendix 2

The following is based on ten steps as taught by Pablo Bottari. He is the author of *Free in Christ* (Charisma House, 2000), and this information is used with permission. Having a two-page summary has been very helpful to many in learning to pray for others. I have made some changes that express things I have learned and found valuable in helping people come to freedom.

Ten Steps to Deliverance

Step 1. Evaluate the person to determine if he is really manifesting an evil spirit.

Step 2. Make the evil spirit submit in the name of Jesus.
- Speak to the spirit, "Submit yourself in the name of Jesus."
- Luke 10:17: "Lord, even the demons submit to us in your name."
- Take authority over the spirit, not the person.

Step 3. Have the person open his eyes. Help him regain con-
sciousness or control over his body.
- Don't have a dialogue with demons.
- Talk to the person. Help him to feel safe.
- If necessary say, "(Name), take control of your body and of your mind in the name of Jesus. Open your eyes."

Step 4. Ask the person if he wants to be free. (This is the first step if he has not manifested.)
- He must want deliverance.
- He must make the decision to be free.

Step 5. Ask the person if he is a believer, and:
- If so, continue to next step.
- If not, share the truth of the Gospel and lead him to Christ.
- If he is not willing, do not continue.

Step 6. Interview the person (look for root causes, areas of bondage). Look for roots in:
- The body—sexual sins: heterosexual, homosexual, animals
- The soul—hatred: resentment, envy, pride, vengeance, rage, bitterness, unforgiveness, fear, traumas, fixations, complexes, doubts, insecurity, phobias
- The spiritual—occultism: Ouija boards, horoscopes, psychic hotlines, fortunetellers, tarot cards, witchcraft, divination, black magic, voodoo, curses

Step 7A. Pray with the person, asking Jesus to set him free. Have the person pray a prayer of repentance for sins he acknowledged in the interview, and ask him to pronounce forgiveness to anyone he has not fully forgiven. (He must be willing, but often heartfelt repentance and forgiveness do not take place until after renouncing the area of bondage and breaking the power.)

Step 7B. Have the person renounce each area of bondage. To give up or renounce a specific area of bondage means to withdraw from any engagement, commitment, agreement or covenant the person has made with the enemy, whether physical, mental or spiritual.

- Ask the Holy Spirit to bring to mind important details.
- Have the person be specific.
- Have him say it in a clear and firm voice.

Some samples of pronouncements:

Physical Bondage

- "In the name of Jesus I renounce all sexual and spiritual binding with (name of person), and I also renounce the authority I gave to him/her."

Bondage of Hatred

- "In the name of Jesus I renounce all bondage of hatred I have against (name of person), and I forgive him for (state the specific experience) in the name of Jesus."

Bondage of Fear

- "In the name of Jesus I renounce all bondage of fear that came upon me" (give reason or name of person who caused fear). If someone caused the fear, forgive and bless the person in the name of Jesus.

Spiritual Bondage

- "In the name of Jesus I renounce the authority I gave over my life to (name of fortuneteller, soothsayer, witch, sorcerer, enchanter or wizard) and to the spirit that operated in (name of sorcerer)."
- For general areas of oppression have the person renounce freely anything he seeks freedom from. "In the name of Jesus I renounce lust, fear, unforgiveness, deception, manipulation, control, fantasy, self-pity . . ."

Relational Bondage

- "In the name of Jesus I break every unholy tie to (name the person—that is, Mother, Father, old boyfriend) and I take responsibility for my life."

Step 8A. Break the power of all spirits.
- When necessary, the minister may say after each specific area of renunciation, "I break this bondage in the name of Jesus."

Step 8B. Cast out the unclean spirits.
- Say, "In the name of Jesus I command every spirit to leave now."
- If the person starts to manifest again, go back to steps 2, 3 and 6.
- If there is no relief, go back to step 6, the interview.

Step 9. Lead the person in a prayer of thanksgiving for his deliverance.
- A good way to do this is to have him lift his hands and say, "Thank You, Jesus, for setting me free."

Step 10. Pray for the person to be newly filled with the Holy Spirit, and speak words of blessing and acceptance over him.

- Lead the person in a prayer such as, "Now I receive the filling of the Holy Spirit and give the glory to You, my Lord."
- If he is not totally free, go back to steps 2, 3 and 6.

Give the person instruction, encouragement, warning and direction to help him cooperate with the grace of God so he will remain free. Now that he has been set free, he is free to make the right choices. Now he can develop a new pattern of behavior and thinking that is built daily by trusting in Jesus, making the right choices, repenting quickly and living in the light as a follower of Jesus among the fellowship of believers.

If the person has not already done so, he must cleanse his house, destroying anything that represents the kingdom of darkness. Anything that was used in satanic practice must be destroyed.

Notes

Introduction

1. I tell my story in my first book, *The Older Brother Returns*.

2. I have not dealt directly with the biblical and theological reasons why one would believe in the devil. Nor have I written a defense of prayer for deliverance. Many others have done that. The reality of the devil is a thread that flows through this book as I quote the Scriptures and tell the stories of those who have been liberated. When I refer to the devil or evil spirits, I am not speaking metaphorically. I am referring to a real, diabolical being or host of beings that have actual identities.

3. Defining of terms: 1) When I use the term deliverance I am referring to deliverance from the influence of evil spirits, not the broader meaning of salvation. 2) What has become widely known as "deliverance prayer" is technically not prayer, that is, conversation with God. It is often referred to as prayer because everything that happens is in the context of prayer, asking Jesus the Deliverer to come. 3) Finally, when referring to deliverance as ministry, I mean the act of serving, cooperating with the Holy Spirit, sharing in the ministry of Jesus. For some Christians this is enough to establish them in a ministry, but for most a ministry can be established only within the context of the Church and through appropriate authority.

Chapter 1

1. Except for my wife and son, who wanted to share with you what they have learned, all the names have been changed along with some circumstances to disguise the identities of those whose stories are told.

Chapter 2

1. See *An Expository Dictionary of Biblical Words*, W.E. Vine, Merrill F. Unger, William White, Jr. (Nashville: Thomas Nelson Inc., Publishers, 1984), 283.

2. At a recent seminar we prayed with almost thirty people. Only one person began to manifest in response to ministry. I suspect this happened because he had been going though deliverance for some time and had expectations of how he would be set free.

3. C. S. Lewis, *The Screwtape Letters* (New York: Simon & Schuster, 1961), 15.

Chapter 3

1. John Paul II, Encyclical Letter Redemptoris Mission, *On the Permanent Validity of the Church's Missionary Mandate* (Washington: Office for Publishing and Promotion Services, United States Catholic Conference, 1990), 78–9.

2. The challenge to put into words what one has done wrong is one of the great gifts of the sacrament of reconciliation in the Catholic tradition. When I am ministering to Catholics, I view the process of deliverance from the influence of evil spirits as preparation for that liberating encounter with God. Many have told me that after deliverance prayer, they made the most honest and significant confession of their lives.

Chapter 4

1. Desmond Tutu, *South Africa: No Future Without Forgiveness* (New York: Doubleday, 1999), 270–71.

2. A year later I contacted Lydia about using her story. "I have forgiven my parents," she declared and in freedom remembers them with gratitude. She added that since we saw her, "two of my children have already forgiven me and thanked me for giving life to them."

3. This is certainly something each of us can do by ourselves, every time it is needed. For deeper forgiveness it is helpful to have someone pray with us as I have suggested. If the situation with the person you need to forgive has created emotional, psychological or spiritual instability, you may wish to find someone with more experience and become familiar with the rest of this book before proceeding.

Chapter 5

1. It is not always necessary to know if you are simply renouncing a lie you have believed or an evil spirit behind the lie. You will know if a spirit was involved when you are released. In the case of Jamie, she renounced a number of things but faced her spiritual bondage when she named rejection.

Chapter 6

1. Knowing Jesus includes recognizing His body, honoring the Lord in His body, the Church, and being in proper relationship to those God has placed in authority in the Church. Isolated, we are subject to great deception.

2. It is important not to blur the lines between prayer and commands to the devil. If it is a command to the devil, by definition it is no longer a prayer, which can only be addressed to God. In our daily conversations with God we should not give our attention to the devil. One of the underlying principles of this book is that the process of deliverance from evil spirits does not need to focus on demons. Be careful not to fall into patterns of prayer or thoughts that focus on demons.

Chapter 7

1. J. I. Packer, *Knowing God* (Downers Grove, Ill.: InterVarsity Press, 1973), 41.

Chapter 10

1. Craig Hill, *The Ancient Paths* (Littleton, Colo: Family Foundations Publishing, 1992), 49.

2. Deliverance ministry will always be incomplete if not placed in the context of normal Christian living. For many years Fr. Michael Scanlan has made the case that deliverance from evil spirits should be a regular part of the sacrament of reconciliation as practiced in the Catholic Church. I believe it should also be part of the initiation process, small groups (friends helping friends), discipleship training, spiritual counseling and pastoral care.

3. Catholic Standard and Times, "It Was No Exorcism," Sept. 13, 2001.

4. If you have begun your reading with this chapter, I encourage you to prayerfully consider reading the first nine chapters for your own benefit.

5. I would like to mention three in particular. From the book *Deliverance from Evil Spirits* by Fr. Mike Scanlan and Randall Cirner, I learned the basics of deliverance. Its emphasis on a solid pastoral approach is the best I have read. From Freedom in Christ by Pablo Bottari from Argentina, I saw wisdom brought forth with simplicity and compassion. I have had the privilege of knowing these authors personally. A third book is Deliverance from Evil Spirits by Francis MacNutt, who has been a pioneer in deliverance ministry. This book is a complete and well-balanced manual. It touches almost all the accumulated wisdom of the past thirty years. Caution: Be careful not to collect unnecessary baggage associated with a particular person's style of prayer ministry. I recommend keeping it simple and seeking to understand the necessary principles as you try to help people. Let God teach you through continued study and reflection. I know many people who have read books on deliverance and never helped a friend get free. I know of others who attempt to make universal laws out of something unique to an individual approach. The benefit of these books and many others is that each author reveals a part of the wisdom God is giving to His people.

6. Francis MacNutt, in his book *Deliverance from Evil Spirits*, speaks a warning worth heeding: "[But] those drawn to praying for deliverance are often impetuous, snap-judgment personalities—precisely the kinds of people who should not be praying for deliverance. The tragedy is they do not know their weakness" (p. 148). He continues that those who minister deliverance to others should be mature Christians "who combine a simple faith with an awareness of difficul-

ties; someone who can join a knowledge of psychology and human frailty with the exercise of the gifts of the Holy Spirit (like discernment). Such a mature person is always prepared to pray for deliverance" (p. 149). I would add that this knowledge may be instinctive and learned through observation and experience as well as training.

Chapter 12

1. My adaptation of his ten-step method is in Appendix 2. For a full explanation I recommend *Free in Christ* by Pablo Bottari (Charisma House, 2000).

Chapter 13

1. This is what I would consider the norm for a person who is in need of or seeking deliverance. If it is simple oppression, a much simpler approach to helping the person repent, forgive, renounce, command and receive blessing may be taken. For example, if someone has already been set free yet begins to be harassed and tempted, he may need simple follow-up prayer strengthening him in what he has already received.

2. Sometimes it is helpful to have a person fill out a questionnaire before coming for prayer. This will keep you from missing the obvious. I have reprinted one in Appendix 1, from Francis MacNutt's book *Deliverance from Evil Spirits*.

3. Many people may be blind to the danger of occult practice and the warning of the Scriptures:

"When you enter the land the Lord your God is giving you, do not learn to imitate the detestable ways of the nations there. Let no one be found among you who sacrifices his son or daughter in the fire, who practices divination of sorcery, interprets omens, engages in witchcraft, or cast spells, or who is a medium or spiritist or who consults the dead." (Deuteronomy 18:9–11).

"He sacrificed his sons in the fire in the valley of Ben Hinnom, practiced sorcery, divination and witchcraft, and consulted mediums and spiritists (2 Chronicles 33:6). He did much evil in the eyes of the Lord, provoking him to anger."

Occult practice is a violation of the first commandment, "You shall have no other gods before Me." You should be prepared to explain how the enemy would use sincere people and half-truths to deceive people, seeking to divert the reverence and honor that belongs to God alone.

4. Some teach that you should not touch the person. I believe this is a deception based on fear and a focus on demons. If you have authority to pray for a person, you can touch them without fear. As instruments of God's love we are protected. Others on the team, however, should not touch the persons because their position on the team is not an expression of the Lord's authority, but of intercession, discernment and support.

5. If the person is Catholic, you must consider his conscience and the grace that is available to him in the sacrament of reconciliation. Depending on a number of factors, you may encourage him to receive the sacrament of reconciliation before continuing, or encourage him to confess his sins now, making the intention to receive the grace of the sacrament in the near future.

6. Preliminary statements in the New Rite of Exorcism in the Catholic church stress the role of the ordained clergy in deliverance ministry as well as the formal Rite of Exorcism. Only priests with proper authorization of the bishop can perform an official exorcism using the formal rite, which is designated for use only in the most extreme cases. With the exception of a statement issued by the Congregation for the Doctrine of the Faith on September 29, 1984, to deter making public display of demonic manifestation and the practice of dialoguing with demons (seeking to discover their identities), there is to my knowledge no further restriction on lay Catholics in the area of simple deliverance. The implication of these preliminary statements is that there may be restrictions in the future. This is a time of consultation and dialogue with local bishops that will lead to local pastoral directives to clarify what belongs to the realm of the ordained clergy and what is in the hands of those who exercise the gift of discernment of spirits (see 1 Corinthians 12:10) and function in accordance with the authority they have been given as believers. "And these signs will accompany those who believe: In my name they will drive out demons" (Mark 16:17).

Index

Neal Lozano, with a master's degree in religious education, has more than thirty-five years of pastoral experience helping people find freedom in Christ. As founders of Heart of the Father Ministries, Neal and his wife, Janet, travel both nationally and internationally, bringing the message of *Unbound* in training seminars and conferences.

Neal, a Roman Catholic, is also the senior coordinator of the House of God's Light, an interdenominational Christian community that he has pastored for thirty-five years.

His first book, *The Older Brother Returns*, (Attic Studio Press, 1995) explains the hidden sins of the heart, inviting the reader to receive the gift of repentance.

Neal has also written the Will You Bless Me? Series which is comprised of three children's books. These tender stories speak to the hearts of parents and children alike revealing the importance and power of the spoken blessing.

He has also served as the director of Renewal and Reconciliation, an association of churches in the greater Philadelphia region.

Neal and Janet have four grown sons and seven grandchildren.

For more information about Unbound Freedom in Christ conferences or other resources, please visit the Heart of the Father Ministries website:

www.heartofthefather.com
email info@heartofthefather.com